The I Am In Me Part 2

The I Am In Me Part 2

You are Precious to God, 2nd Edition

Tekisha D Wimbush

J Merrill Publishing, Inc.
434 Hillpine Drive
Columbus, OH 43207
www.JMerrill.pub

Library of Congress Control Number: 2022913797
ISBN-13: 978-1-954414-52-5 (Paperback)
ISBN-13: 978-1-954414-51-8 (eBook)

Book Title: The I Am In Me Part 2, You are Precious to God, 2nd Edition
Author: Tekisha D. Wimbush

Table of Contents

Acknowledgments   ix

Introduction   xi

1. The Stage Has Already Been Set, Just Play The Role   1
2. Hello, Hello; What Are You Doing In Your Dash Dash?   7
3. Pray About Everything; Worry About Nothing   15
4. I'm Looking For My Miracle   23
5. We Had a Problem, But I Got a Right: A Personal Rant   29
6. I Won't Bow; I'm Taking a Stand in Jesus   35
7. It's Time to Lift Up Jesus; It's Time to Raise Up Your Praise   43
8. There Is Peace after the Storm!   51
9. Raise Up Your Standard; There's a Price Tag for the Anointing   57
10. I'm not in that place anymore; God has moved me   65
11. My God Answers by Fire!   71
12. Are You Spiritually and Naturally Fit? Allow Me to Heal   79
13. In Pursuit of My Happiness   85
14. Because God has left His Imprint upon Me   91
15. It's Time To Make A Change   97
16. Off The Grid   103
17. Out of the Belly of the Beast   109
18. Let Our Devotion Be Pleasing to God As we Seek Him   117
19. I Came to Bless Him   123
20. I Speak Life   129
21. I Am Built for This   137
22. Favor after Failure   143
23. I have the More— But only if I Believe   149

24. My God is a Progressive God: Let's Move Forward   157
25. Praise is Usual (My Praise); It's not Uncommon   163
26. Man Closes Doors, But So Do You   171
27. God Changed My Name   177
28. The Only Thing That Stands between Me and
Victory Is Me   183

About the Author   189

A Path to Your best self through Christ

Acknowledgments

Thank You to our Lord and Savior, Jesus Christ. God is Good! He is Me- methodical in all that he Does! Thank You to all the supporters of Part 1 of "The I Am In Me." Because God is Methodical, I now present Part 2! Thank You to my family, friends, and loved ones. To my Best Friend - My husband, Bishop Willie J. Wimbush Jr., and my children Jasemine, Jaden, and Jahdon, who makes me so proud. My two grandchildren, Brandon and Bella, keep me on my toes! My mother, Pastor Shawyl R. Williams, my Loving Church Family Church of the Reform Church of Love, Majennie Creations LLC, Focused Dreamers LLC/Non-Profit, and the Sister 2 Sister Focus Group, all of whom push me to greater heights and depths of exploration to gain further in-depth wisdom, knowledge, and understanding that I may be the Best Me in efforts to Lead and Support Others.

Introduction

As you continue to live, you will find that to grow for the better; you Must do the Work. Presented with the tools to do so is separate from one doing the work. I discovered that although I have numerous bibles and technical gadgets, it means nothing if I do not read with the ability to comprehend and understand to engage in the application process. What separates the elite is they do not lose the desire to:

1. Comprehend
2. Understand
3. Application

All three are profitable for spiritual, natural, physical, and mental growth. Self-Examination is KEY to measuring the right application of the word of God and Spiritual Growth, and what better way to do that than reading the WORD? The I Am In Me Part 2 is a tool to help examine life application while engaging the reader to apply the WORD! Let's Do the Work that we feed the Spirit Man, Grow in

Introduction

God, Starve& Beat Our Flesh Daily, Advance the Kingdom, Witness to Others, Deny our Selves, and Seek Ye First the Kingdom of God!

Chapter 1
The Stage Has Already Been Set, Just Play The Role

1st Kings 2:1-12 and 2nd Timothy 3:16-17

We understand that the word "stage" has several meanings or definitions. Today, we will look at the word's noun form: A raised floor or platform, typically in a theater, on which actors, entertainers, or speakers perform. We will also look at its verb form: To write, direct, or produce (a play) with the action taking place as if in a specified locale or time. To stage, then, is to plan, organize, or carry out (an activity), especially for dramatic public effect.

When we look at the word "stage" in our lesson text, we discover that the Stage has already been set. The characters and roles have already been assigned; the only thing left is acting out the parts. We see David, the character in this passage of 1st Kings, in the role of transitioning, or "passing away," if you will. We are leaving the earth to a new state of being. The stage is set; as written, David's character carries a strong storyline. This lead character, spoken of in both the

Old and New Testaments, evolves into a "Man after God's Own Heart" throughout the books of the Bible. From the child that cared for the sheep to the anointed successor of King Saul. From hero to adulterer, to murderer, to penitent.

He is now speaking with the next leader, Solomon, son of David, expressing to him the vitality of his role and the importance of his ability to execute the duties of his position. David lays out the script calling for a lead man, presenting Solomon with the plan of organization that must be carried out. David gives him the charge of keeping God's laws and ensuring that God remains the center of his life and government to ensure that the Kingdom is preserved (1st Kings 2:1-4):

> Now the days of David drew nigh that he should die; and he charged Solomon his son, saying, I go the way of all the earth: be thou strong, therefore, and shew thyself a man; And keep the charge of the Lord thy God, to walk in his ways, to keep his statutes, and his commandments, and his judgments, and his testimonies, as it is written in the law of Moses, that thou mayest prosper in all that thou doest, and whithersoever thou turnest thyself: That the Lord may continue his word which he spake concerning me, saying, If thy children take heed to their way, to walk before me in truth with all their heart and with all their soul, there shall not fail thee (said he) a man on the throne of Israel.

We find out that the script written by unknown authors here in 1st Kings suggested the presence of prophets to contrast the lives of those who live for God and those who refuse to do so throughout the history of the kings of Israel and Judah. Part of this setting lets us know that Israel's once great nation devolved into a physically and spiritually divided land. If we look around, it reminds us of our once-allegedly great nation, the United States of America.

How many of us know that the promises of God come with conditions? Remember why the WORD—the SCRIPT—was given, and who gave it to us: (2nd Timothy 3:16-17), thus setting our stage.

All scripture is given by inspiration of God, and is profitable for doctrine, for reproof, for correction, for instruction in righteousness:

The scriptures. The breathed word of God, given by inspiration of God. The plan that requires us to read it to observe the stage is that we might interpret the script to apply and act out our role in the manner given by the Director. In creating movies, the directors yell "CUT!" when the actors go off the script. They yell "CUT!" when the actors deviate from their assigned character roles. Part of this walk in God requires that "YOU KNOW WHO YOU ARE." That you are aligned with His will and in His place. Take your places, everyone!

In 1st Kings, particular lines in the script outlined the conditions of God's promise in two parts. The first part was conditional and relied upon the King's ability to play the role, as the stage was already set. Is it not Samuel who says, "to obey is better than sacrifice" (1st Samuel 15:22)? The script of the conditional promise stated that David and his descendants would remain in the office (Place) of King as long as they abided by the laws of God (Script), mainly to obey and honor God (Role Play). If you read on to 2nd Kings chapter 25, however, we find out that the Kings failed to adhere to the given conditions, and thus by going off script, they lost their throne. "CUT!" This is why you must stick with the script. Stay in character on the stage already set before you, and play the role you have been given. We don't want to be blackballed from the industry and classified as hard to work with! "...depart from me...."

The other part was unconditional. We understand that God promised David that his bloodline would live on forever. Because God does not lie, and He does not renege on His promises, as scripted by Paul in Romans 1:2-4:

> *Which he had promised afore by his prophets in the*
> *holy scriptures, Concerning his Son Jesus Christ*
> *our Lord, which was made of the seed of David*
> *according to the flesh;*
> *And declared to be the Son of God with power,*
> *according to the spirit of holiness, by the*
> *resurrection from the dead: By whom we have*
> *received grace and apostleship, for obedience to*
> *the faith among all nations, for his name:*
> *Obedience to the faith sets the pretense that the*
> *stage has already been set and you must play the*
> *role.*

We have God in character, manifested in human nature through the descendants of David. The Jewish royal bloodline appears in the role of Jesus, who died and rose from the dead—thereby setting the stage, making way for us to have fellowship with God. Just play the role!

_____
_____
_____
_____
_____
_____
_____
_____
_____

" SO GOODBYE SELF, AND HELLO JOY, HELLO PEACE, HELLO LOVE, FROM THE OTHER SIDE. I'M ON THE OTHER SIDE OF GUILT, THE OTHER SIDE OF SHAME, THE OTHER SIDE OF REMORSE, THE OTHER SIDE OF POVERTY.

Chapter 2
Hello, Hello; What Are You Doing In Your Dash Dash?
Hebrews 9:27; Ecclesiastes 3:1-8

Hebrews 9:27; Ecclesiastes 3:1-8

The words Hello and Dash are significant for "Reflective Thoughts."

Hello, Hello! I'm just laying a canvas here. Admittedly a bit unorthodox— which I thought meant unusual, out of the ordinary, peculiar, out of order, or otherwise just flat-out weird—but painting a picture all the same. In the words of the late Tupac Shakur, "Picture Perfect, I Paint a Perfect Picture." Consider these words from (1st Corinthians 27):

> *But God hath chosen the foolish things of the world to*
> *confound the wise; and God hath chosen the weak*
> *things of the world to confound the things which*
> *uses the foolish things to confound the things*
> *which are mighty.*

Four words of Significant Fruit for Thought today:

1. Hello, Hello: A salutation is defined as a greeting or a response (e.g., when on the phone). Also used to bring attention or as an expression of surprise. Sometimes sarcastically used to get one's attention— "Hellooo!?"—often posed as a question.
2. Dash (-): Visualized as a small 'minus sign,' signifying a break or pause.
3. Reflection: Meditation or serious thought about one's own character, actions, and/or motives.
4. Self: A person's essential being that distinguishes them from others. Considered the object of introspection or reflectiveness. (dictionary.com)

We know, according to David, that "God is perfecting those things concerning me" (Psalms 138:8). Point to yourself and say, "Me!" While we have dreams, God has a plan and a will for us. This is why we must "Keep thy heart with all diligence; for out of it are the issues of life" (Proverbs 4:23)—our heart, our feelings of love and desire— which dictates how we act and live.

The songwriter Adele's song "Hello" is rated high in the genre of pop/ soul. When I first listened to it, there was something different about it, something mystifying that caught my attention: Firstly, her captivating voice; secondly, the beautiful instruments; thirdly, the lyrics. This led me to research the song further and dig deeper into the meaning of the lyrics. Why am I even interested to know? Why would God prompt me to investigate this song? What is the significance? While the video provides a visual reflection of a relationship between two individuals that have gone bad, the lyrics have a subliminal message (defined as a stimulus that lies below our threshold of conscious awareness - dictionary.com). Because they fall below our absolute threshold level, we can't perceive such a message, even if we're looking for it. This is important, as many people confuse subliminal influence with subconscious influence.

Hello, it's me
I was wondering if after all these years you'd like to meet
To go over everything
They say that time's supposed to heal ya, but I ain't done much healing

Hello, can you hear me?
I'm in California dreaming about who we used to be
When we were younger and free
I've forgotten how it felt before the world fell at our feet

There's such a difference between us
And a million miles

Hello from the other side

I must've called a thousand times
To tell you I'm sorry for everything that I've done
But when I call, you never seem to be home

Hello from the outside
At least I can say that I've tried
To tell you I'm sorry for breaking your heart
But it don't matter, it clearly doesn't tear you apart anymore

Hello, how are you?
It's so typical of me to talk about myself, I'm sorry
I hope that you're well
Did you ever make it out of that town where nothing ever happened?

It's no secret that the both of us
Are running out of time

Open your mouth, tap yourself, and say, "Hello, Hello, Self! What are you doing in your Dash... Move Self... Deal with Self..." Self-care is essential. Adele is writing about herself; the song depicts "Self." This is significant: Who AM I? Old Self; New Self; Help Self; a reflection of Self; an examination of Self; Self-worth; growth of Self; Self-healing; Self-apology; the forgiveness of Self. The song says, "Hello, it's me"—an introduction of Self, a reconnection, a rebirth, for if any man be in Christ, he is a New Creature. Old things are passed away. Behold all things become new" (2nd Corinthians 5:17). The bible says in Acts 2:40: "Peter preached to the crowd, Save yourselves from this untoward generation." In the next verse, Acts 2:41, we understand that after Self-reflection and Self-examination, those that gladly received the word were baptized in the name of Jesus and received the Holy Ghost, and so that day, 3,000 souls were added to the church.

So Hello, Hello from the other side; Hello from the outside, Hello from the inside out—Jesus is on the inside of me (Holy Ghost), and he is roaring like a lion. So goodbye, Self, and Hello Joy, Hello Peace, Hello Love, from the other side. I'm on the other side of guilt, the other side of shame, the other side of remorse, and the other side of poverty. Hello! Now that I have your attention, the question is: What are you doing in your Dash?

Hello, Hello! Like Adele, we all need to say Hello, Hello to Salvation (Jude 24-25):

> Now unto him that is able to keep you from falling,
>   and to present you faultless before the presence of
>   his glory with exceeding joy, To the only wise God
>   our Saviour, be glory and majesty, dominion and
>   power, both now and ever. Amen.

Hello, Hello! While I have your attention in this moment of Self-reflection, my name is Tekisha D. Wimbush, born January 26, 1976-(Dash). Right now, there is a dash—a pause, clarifying a span of time, a dispensation of time. I have time to do what God requires before he imposes judgment. Hello, Hello! What are you doing in your Dash? We all have an appointed date of expiration—a Dash. But what are you doing in your Dash? "But No man knows the hour...."

Hello, Hello! Have you repented? Have you been baptized? The Bible says that the kingdom of God is at hand. Hello, Hello! What are you doing in your Dash? What are you doing in your dispensation of Grace during your Grace Period? Hello! Have you received the Holy Ghost since you believed? Hello! Are you a witness? Are you telling somebody that Jesus saves!?

Hello, Hello!

_____
_____
_____
_____
_____
_____
_____
_____
_____
_____
_____
_____
_____
_____
_____
_____
_____
_____

I SHALL NOT CONTINUE IN SIN, THAT GRACE MAY THUS NOT ABOUND. SIN HAS NO RULE; THE SPIRIT OF THE LORD CAME TO SET US FREE. IT'S UP TO YOU TO ACCEPT IT!

Chapter 3
Pray About Everything; Worry About Nothing

A simple, short "Thought"
Prayer: My communication "Petitions unto God"
Proverbs 15:29

The LORD is far from the wicked:
but he heareth the prayer of the righteous.

Wicked (adj.): Evil or morally bad in principle or practice;
sinful; iniquitous Righteous (adj.): (of a person or conduct)
Morally right or justifiable; virtuous (www.dictionary.com).
The last time we met, we said that the "Effectual fervent
prayer of the righteous availeth much."
Effectual (adj.): Yielding a desired result
Fervent (adj.): Burning with fire; having earnest passion or
aspirations
(www.dictionary.com).

We, therefore, understand the scripture, James 5:16, when James says: "Confess your faults one to another, and pray one for another, that Ye may be healed."

I SHALL NOT CONTINUE IN SIN, THAT GRACE MAY THUS NOT ABOUND. SIN HAS NO RULE; THE SPIRIT OF THE LORD CAME TO SET US FREE. IT'S UP TO YOU TO ACCEPT IT!

Pray about everything; worry about nothing.

In this life, we have all kinds of navigational instruments and other research tools to measure or analyze an actual or predicted outcome. We also have all types of career paths. If you register for courses in the study of nursing, follow the course outline through graduation after three years, then take a state exam and successfully pass it, then Behold, you are now a licensed practical nurse (LPN). You could then acquire your Bachelor of Nursing (BSN), thus extending your course work to a 4-year term and passing a licensure test to become a registered nurse (RN)— all with no questions asked.

When we look at navigation in our vehicles, we put in addresses, some of which we have never driven before. We set it with no further regard, and we follow the GPS lady's voice as she reads the road map to our destination. We then arrive feeling accomplished, as our navigation system got us here with no problems. Some of us might even have no idea of the route we took to get to our destination; all we know is that we arrived.

When it comes to spiritual navigation, our Instrument, our Tool, is our Bible, our basic instructions before leaving earth. It is equipped with data that are measured, valid, reliable, and proven to be true. But we struggle along the journey to our destination because of ourselves—our fear, our lack of faith, our plain old unbelief, and our sin.

Isaiah warned us against sin in the Scriptures (Isaiah 59:1):

> *Behold, the Lord's hand is not shortened, that it cannot*
> *save; neither his ear heavy, that he cannot hear:*

Isaiah, son of Amos and one of the major prophets in the bible, writes this book of the bible to call the nation of Judah back to God and to tell of God's salvation through the Messiah. (Jesus Saves!)

"Behold": We know that this means to see or observe a thing or person, especially a remarkable or impressive one. To tell somebody to watch this. "Why, then, does it seem like the Lord does not hear or answer my prayers?" Tell them to check your Instrument. According to our Tool, the Bible, in (Isaiah 59:2) we are told:

> *But your iniquities have separated between you and*
> *your God, and your sins have hid his face from*
> *you, that he will not hear.*

I'm just doing as Isaiah did, as I was commissioned to do: Crying loud and sparing not, having been called to move Self out of the way and submit myself therefore unto God, recognizing that He already sent Jesus in the atonement of our sins, to reconcile us with Him.

Paul asked a question in (Romans 6:1-2):

> *What shall we say then? Shall we continue in sin, that*
> *grace may abound? God forbid.*

Therefore, I shall not continue in sin, that grace may thus not abound. Sin has no rule; the Spirit of the Lord came to set us free. It's up to you to accept it!

If you are healed now in Christ (Romans 8:1-2):

> *There is therefore no condemnation to them which are*
> *in Christ Jesus, who walk not after the flesh, but*
> *after (navigated) by the Spirit. For the law of the*
> *Spirit of life in Christ Jesus hath made me free*
> *from the law of sin and death.*

I can ask what I will of the Lord! I can pray about everything, and "I ain't worryin' about nothin'"! I am casting all my cares upon the Lord, for he careth for me.

(1st Peter 5:7).

Pray about everything; worry about nothing!

_____
_____
_____
_____
_____
_____
_____
_____
_____
_____
_____
_____
_____
_____
_____
_____
_____
_____
_____
_____
_____
_____
_____
_____
_____
_____
_____
_____
_____

"I EXPECT THE IMPOSSIBLE; I FEEL THE
INTANGIBLE; I SEE THE INVISIBLE; THE SKY
IS THE LIMIT"

Tekisha D Wimbush

"Sin has no rule. The spirit of the Lord came to set us free."

Chapter 4
I'm Looking For My Miracle

I felt like toast this morning—dry, tired, brittle. But God! I'm looking for my miracle!

What is a miracle?

Miracle is attributed to a (n.): An event not able to be accounted for or understood by natural or scientific laws. Such an event may be attributed to a supernatural being (God or gods), a miracle worker, a saint, or a religious leader.

I'm looking for my miracle: A demonstration of the power of God in my life.

Consider the words in 1st Samuel 1:1-20. Do we have any Samuels in here today? His name meant "something you have asked of the Lord." I'm looking for my miracle. I have asked the Lord for my miracle; I have asked the Lord to look upon my afflictions, whatever my problem is, whatever my situation is, and I have asked the Lord to remember me in my circumstances. I have made my petition; now I'm looking for my miracle.

Miracle (n.): A supernatural direct intervention by God in this world in your life.

I'm looking for my miracle. The legendary Clark Sisters said, "I expect the impossible; I feel the intangible; I see the invisible; the sky is the limit." I'm looking for my miracle. I'm looking for my supernatural intervention from God. For "faith is the substance of things hoped for, the evidence of things not seen" (Hebrews 11:1).

I'm looking for my miracle.

> *"But as it is written, Eye hath not seen, nor ear heard, neither have entered into the heart of man, the things which God hath prepared for them that love him."*
>
> — (1st Cor. 2:9)

I'm looking for my miracle.

> *"There are many devices in a man's heart; nevertheless the counsel of the Lord, that shall stand."*
>
> — (Proverbs 19:21)

I'm looking for my miracle.

> *"For I know the thoughts that I think toward you, saith the Lord, thoughts of peace, and not of evil, to give you an expected end."*
>
> — (Jeremiah 29:11)

That doesn't mean you won't go through some trials. But God will be there all the way through. He said He's coming like a thief in the night, and His reward is with Him. I'm looking for my miracle!

_____

_____

_____

_____

_____

_____

_____

_____

_____

_____

_____

_____

_____

_____

_____

_____

_____

_____

_____

_____

_____

_____

_____

_____

_____

_____

Tekisha D Wimbush

_____
_____
_____
_____
_____
_____
_____
_____
_____
_____
_____
_____
_____
_____
_____
_____
_____
_____
_____
_____
_____
_____
_____
_____

 I WILL LIFT YOU UP FROM THE FRUIT OF MY LIPS THE DEPTHS OF MY HEART.

"He's coming like a thief in the night, and His reward is with Him."

Chapter 5
We Had a Problem, But I Got a Right: A Personal Rant

If I had never had a problem, I wouldn't know God could solve it. I'd never know He could answer prayers, that he could answer by fire, that He could deliver me. If I never had a problem that I identified, I'd never know who God is. I have a right to lift Him up; I have a right to give God praise, for He solved all my problems and supplied all my needs.

I have a right to tell him, "Thank You." I have a right to send up Judah, for He is worthy of my praise; He's due honor in my worship. I have a right! On Calvary, he gave me the right! O I believe I've confessed with my mouth; I've tarried; I've received that Holy Ghost power; I've gone down in the name of Jesus and come back up in the newness of life. I got a right!

The world didn't give it, and the world can't take it away. God gave me the right, through Christ Jesus, to serve Him, to praise Him, to worship Him in spirit and in truth. My worship is for real! I've got a right! To lift Him higher, to praise Him harder, O I got a right!

You can't hinder me; you can't stop me; you can't block me. I got a right. To enter into His gates with thanksgiving and into His courts with praise. To praise him on the stringed instruments, on the high-sounding cymbals, to let everything that has breath praise. Praise, praise, praise ye the Lord, for He is worthy; He is worthy; he is worthy to be praised! He is highly lifted up!

You have been served; you got your notification. Well, this is my response: My problems are not greater than my praise. God did that. I got a right!

Smile, God, smile, for He inhabits the praises of His people. The smile on my life, O God, for you gave me the right! I am grateful, O God, that you didn't leave me in my sin, in my iniquities, or transgressions; instead, You gave me another chance. You solved the problem, took hold of my sins and took them all the way to the cross, and left them there.

God, I thank you for the right! Lord, I thank you for the Right! Thank you, Jesus, Thank you, Jesus, for the right! Problem solved! I got a right! Where I go, I've got a right to tell Him thank you! I've got a right to count my privileges, to show You honor, to magnify You, to lift You up from the fruit of my lips and the depths of my heart. I got a right! O, that men would praise Me, O, that men would lift Me up! Higher! Higher! I would draw all men into Me.

I got a right!

_____

_____

_____

_____

_____

_____

_____

_____

_____

_____

_____

_____

_____

_____

_____

_____

_____

_____

_____

_____

_____

_____

_____

_____

_____

_____

_____

_____

_____

_____

_____

_____

_____

_____

_____

_____

_____

_____

 "TO EVERYTHING THERE IS A SEASON, AND
A TIME TO EVERY PURPOSE UNDER THE

HEAVEN."

"You gave me another chance."

Chapter 6
I Won't Bow; I'm Taking a Stand in Jesus

Esther 1:1-2, 1:10-13 (Characters: Ahasuerus, Vashti) Esther 2:1-7
(Characters: Vashti, Ahasuerus, Mordecai, Haddasah, i.e., Esther)
Others (Haman, Two Chamberlains: Bigthana and Teresh) Acts
5:29-32

The author of the book of Esther is unknown, although some speculate that Mordecai, Ezra, or possibly Nehemiah may have been the authors. The book describes specific individuals who refused to bow. We understand that the book of Esther represents the sovereignty of God, exemplifying his supreme power and authority. In the words of Dr. Norman Geisler: "Sovereignty is God's control over His creation, dealing with His governance over it: Sovereignty is God's rule over all reality." God has the first and the last say in any given situation. It ain't over 'til God says that it's over!

Esther is one of the two books named after a woman (the other being the book of Ruth). Although in the book of Esther, the unknown author does not explicitly mention God throughout its ten chapters, we understand that He was always there. In our times of need, even when it seems He is far from us, He is always there, for he promised never to leave or forsake us. Some of us have questioned in the great tests, trials, and tribulations—"Lord, where are you?"—not understanding that we are in the depths of our own emotions, as faith tells us that He is there all the time. In our tests, trials, and tribulations, He is there, for He is the bearer of our burdens, our comforter, and our strength. He is our God of sovereignty. If we want to reign with Him, we must suffer with Him.

In suffering with Him, there is a cost, a "price tag" for the anointing. How true this is! You have to be willing to give up something, whether a person, place, or thing, no matter how valuable it is to you. Individuals do not just by luck become anointed; there is a cost, for we understand that God's anointing destroys the yoke of bondage. No one can stand against the anointing; demons tremble at the anointing of God. It's time to get anointed!

There is a saying: "If you don't stand for something, you will fall for anything." And another: "Don't take any wooden nickels." I'm just sounding the alarm. "I like you got something to say": I won't bow; I'm standing in Jesus! I won't bow; I'm standing in Jesus! I won't bow; I'm standing in Jesus! I am standing in the liberty through which Christ has set me free. I. Won't. Bow.

In the book of Esther, we find that some of the characters lifted themselves in their pride, thus placing themselves above others. In retrospect, they were being worshipped as gods—and we know that God said, "he shall have no other Gods before me" (Exodus 20:3). In the very 1st chapter of Esther, we see that King Ahasuerus, who was the king of more than 127 provinces, sat on the throne of the Shushan Palace. While drunk one day, he summoned his chamberlains to request that Queen Vashti come and model her beauty for the all-male audience. However, she refused this request. She refused to bow; without hesitation, she decided to take a stand, despite the adversity she would later face, despite all she had to lose. Well, it cost her: She lost her position as Queen and her royal estate. Yet she was part of God's greater purpose. She may not have realized it at the time, but by taking a stand, she helped pave the way for the Savior to come. "He had to come. He had to come."

Our God is progressive. He is never idle; He is always moving. He is a God of strategic planning; He is methodical; He takes a systematic approach to everything he does in His divine order. Why? Because the Savior had to come from God in the form of a man—the man whom we call "Jesus"—who came from among the Jewish people.

In the 2nd chapter of Esther, there was a certain Jewish man by the name of Mordecai, who raised his uncle's daughter, Hadassah—who was also known as "Esther"—for she had no father and no mother. There goes that "price tag for the anointing" again. There is always a cost for the anointing. Mordecai took in this beautiful young maid for his daughter. We know that she was placed into the custody of Hegai, the keeper of the women. Esther quickly grew in favor with the King. Yet she also held on to her individuality; she did not disclose her true heritage before it was time. Sometimes :

"It's not the time for that yet."

Ecclesiastes 3:1 tells us, "To everything there is a season, and a time to every purpose under the heaven." And it was time for her to be born— about the 10th month, Tebeth, in the 7th year of the King's reign. And as Queen Esther grew, she fell into God's grace, favor, authority, and sovereignty. For she, like Vashti, was destined to help God achieve His purpose. Self Note; "I'm a work in progress; I'm moving forward. I'm leaving my former life behind me so I can press on towards the greater prize of a higher calling in Christ Jesus."

Tekisha D Wimbush

Moving forward, the 3rd chapter describes the promotion of Haman, who was set above all the princes with him. At King Ahasuerus's request, all the king's servants that were at the king's gate bowed and reverenced Haman. "But God, but God." But Mordecai refused to bow to Haman; he refused to give reverence to a man. His refusal placed him and all of his fellow Jews in a difficult situation: His refusal to bow infuriated Haman, thus leading to the casting of lots from day to day, from month to month, as he plotted to destroy all of the Jews. He even went so far as to get permission from the King, with signatures sealed with the King's ring. Letters went out to destroy, kill, and cause all Jews to perish—young, old, little children, and women—in one day! But God always has a ram in the bush: Sometimes, we have to call on our "elders." Mordecai called on Esther for backup.

We then see in the 5th chapter God's divine intervention and purposeful plan in action. Esther stood up in royal apparel, "for we are a royal priesthood, a peculiar people, a chosen generation." She took a "stand in the Lord" in the courts of the King. In so doing, she found favor in his sight. She refused to bow; she stood up for the Jews, the bloodline through which Jesus came. She stood up for her kindred; she stood in Jesus. Mordecai also stood in Jesus; he had faith in God, for he knew that He would bring them out. Throughout the remaining chapters, we see how the king remembered that Mordecai saved his life after two of his chamberlains plotted to kill him. Mordecai made him aware, which led him to grow in favor with the king.

> *"He who exalts himself shall be abased; and he who humbles himself shall be exalted."*
>
> — Matthew 23:12

We see that Haman had a 50-foot-high gallows built to hang Mordecai. "But what the Devil meant for my bad, God turned it around for my good." Haman celebrated Mordecai's death prematurely, for he wound up hanging on the gallows himself.

"Fret not yourself because of evil doers, for they shall be cut off." (Psalms 37) I won't bow; I am standing in Jesus. I am standing on the promises of God. Job stood in Jesus; although he lost everything, he still said, "yet will I trust Him." I won't bow. Even after facing indignation and imprisonment by the Sadducees, Peter and the Apostles stood, declaring that "it is better to obey God than man" (Acts 5:29).

I won't bow. Moses stood, refusing to bow to Pharaoh. He stood and delivered the children of Israel out of bondage. Noah refused to bow; he stood, declaring it was going to rain. The three Hebrew boys refused to bow. Daniel refused to bow. I refuse to bow! I'm standing to see the salvation of the Lord; I am standing for holiness. Stand up for righteousness!

Tekisha D Wimbush

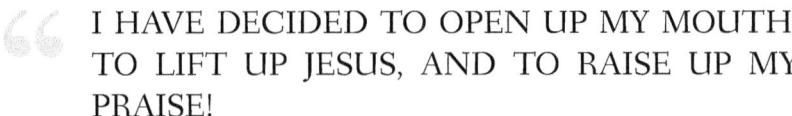

I HAVE DECIDED TO OPEN UP MY MOUTH, TO LIFT UP JESUS, AND TO RAISE UP MY PRAISE!

"I am standing in Jesus."

Chapter 7
It's Time to Lift Up Jesus; It's Time to Raise Up Your Praise

"We are building!" My Pastor once told his congregants that it was time to rebuild. When rebuilding, you must ensure that your foundation is solid. You must address all concerns, issues, circumstances, and problems. When problem-solving, you must first identify the problem and then take the necessary steps to solve it, taking care not to become a part of the problem yourself.

Oftentimes we use the word "priming" to describe preparations for a task.

> Prime (v.t.): www.dictionary.com. To prepare or make ready for a particular purpose or operation.
> Priming (n.): APA Dictionary of Psychology. The effect in which recent experience of a stimulus facilitates or inhibits later processing of the same or a similar stimulus.

An individual has to be stimulated as part of the preparation for a particular purpose. Likewise, notice how the saints needed to be primed, via the stimuli of their life experiences, into a higher purpose of praising God. When we think of praise, your praise should be chronic, meaning all the time, and not acute, which is short-term, here and there, so that you can facilitate a lifetime of praise. I'm always ready to acknowledge the Lord in all His ways! I'm always prepared to magnify Him and lift Him up!

Scripture reading: Book of Joshua

Joshua was Israel's leader at the crossing of the river Jordan into the Promised Land. Chapter 23, in particular, gives us instruction and encouragement on how we can "cleave unto the Lord your God" (Joshua 23:8). He gave specific instructions for the people: (1) To follow the statutes instituted by God through Moses; (2) No intermixing with heathen nations (idolaters, unbelievers, skeptics, atheists) or worshiping their idols; (3) Do not marry within heathen nations. In the 24th chapter, Joshua addresses the people in reflection on their forefathers from the time of the Great Flood. He reminded them of what God had blessed them with and the provisions God made for them when He brought them out of bondage.

It's time to lift up Jesus; it's time to raise your praise!

> 13 *And I have given you a land for which ye did not labour, and cities which ye built not, and ye dwell in them; of the vineyards and oliveyards which ye planted not do ye eat.*
> 14 *Now therefore fear the LORD, and serve him in sincerity and in truth: and put away the gods which your fathers served on the other side of the flood, and in Egypt; and serve ye the LORD.*
> 15 *And if it seem evil unto you to serve the LORD, choose you this day whom ye will serve; whether the gods which your fathers served that were on the other side of the flood in the old time or the*

*gods of the Amorites, in whose land ye dwell: but
as for me and my house, we will serve the LORD.*

— (Joshua 24:13-15, KJV)

Joshua gave the people a choice, but he had already made his decision — as I have made mine. I have decided to open up my mouth, lift up Jesus, and raise my praise! As for me and my house, we will serve the Lord! Let everything that has breath praise ye, O Lord!

What will you do?

Choose Whom You Will Serve (e.g., Deuteronomy 10:12-22)

So, think of the goodness of Jesus and all He's done for you. Then you should already be stimulated to magnify the Lord. For there will not be any priming in Heaven. So, we have to get this right now, in this rehearsal that we call life.

It's time to lift up Jesus; it's time to raise your praise! At the prediction of his death, Jesus said in John 12:32;

*"And I, if I be lifted up from the earth, will draw all
men unto me."*

James referenced this declaration in his letter: "Submit yourselves therefore to God... Draw nigh to God, and he will draw nigh to you." (James 4:7-8, KJV)

It's time to lift up Jesus; it's time to raise your praise!

The scripture says, "Oh that men would praise the LORD for his goodness, and for his wonderful works to the children of men!" (Psalms 107:8) "But thou art holy, O thou that inhabitest the praises of Israel" (Psalms 22:3). Praise is what I do; throughout this journey that we call life.

I will praise ye, O Lord! It's time to take a position in God; it's time to lift Him up. It's time to keep His commandments; it's time to magnify the Lord!

> 9 *Let love be without dissimulation. Abhor that which is evil; cleave to that which is good.*
> 10 *Be kindly affectioned one to another with brotherly love; in honour preferring one another;*
> 11 *Not slothful in business; fervent in spirit; serving the Lord;*
> 12 *Rejoicing in hope; patient in tribulation; continuing instant in prayer;*
> 13 *Distributing to the necessity of saints; given to hospitality.*
>
> — (Romans 12:9-13, KJV)

_____
_____
_____
_____
_____
_____
_____
_____
_____
_____
_____
_____
_____
_____
_____
_____
_____
_____
_____
_____
_____
_____
_____
_____
_____
_____
_____
_____
_____
_____
_____
_____

THE WORDS OF JESUS HIMSELF, DENOTING THAT HE WILL FREELY GIVE US PEACE—IF WE ARE WILLING TO ACCEPT HIM.

Tekisha D Wimbush

"It's time to magnify the Lord!"

Chapter 8
There Is Peace after the Storm!

Matthew 8:23 18-27 (Jesus was homeless, the disciples were afraid, Jesus had peace)

Peace (n.): www.dictionary.com (1) The normal, nonwarring condition of a nation, group of nations, or the world. (2) Freedom of the mind from annoyance, distraction, anxiety, an obsession, etc.; tranquility; serenity.

When we ponder the word "peace," we typically think of the first definition, which is to say, the absence of war. But internal peace is just as important. Some people would do anything for peace of mind. Scripture tells us, "Thou wilt keep him in perfect peace, whose mind is stayed on thee: because he trusteth in thee" (Isaiah 26:3, KJV). This lets us know that we must trust in Him and in His efforts for our minds to stay on Him. Even amidst chaos and turmoil, there is peace with God. This gives us the understanding that we can have meaningful peace in the very midst of any storm: "Peace I leave with you, my peace I give unto you: not as the world giveth, give I unto you. Let not your heart be troubled, neither let it be afraid" (John 14:27). The words of Jesus Himself, denoting that he will freely give us peace—if we are willing to accept Him.

"Fair Exchange; No Robbery" The Old Cliché seems befitting to consider.

Peace surpasses all understanding. The beautiful thing about peace is that you can have it before, during, or after a storm. The Bible tells us, "For when they shall say, Peace and safety; then sudden destruction cometh upon them, as travail upon a woman with child; and they shall not escape" (1 Thessalonians 5:3, KJV). We are called to understand that although we all want and desire peace, there will be a time for storms in our lives. Storms often come angrily, with a violent force, atmospheric disturbance, strong winds, and usually rain, thunder, lightning, or snow. And sometimes, you can, as in the case of the Disciples, be caught without warning. But even in the midst of all of this, God gives us peace.

For those in doubt, storms are prevalent in our lives: "For we wrestle not against flesh and blood, but against principalities, against powers, against rulers of the darkness of this world, against spiritual wickedness in high places" (Ephesians 6:12, KJV). Storms can cause tumultuous reactions, an uproar, or controversy and often find expression in the noisy outburst of a specified feeling or reaction. Storms can wake up something in you as they prey on your emotions. Storms are specific, as they often have an identified target and/or direction. You could be minding your own business, not bothering anyone, even reading the Word and praising God, and STILL find yourself in a storm! It's not by happenstance that you find yourself in a storm, about to go through a storm, or coming out of a storm. But the way you go through is the way you will come out. If you go in peace, you will have peace, "Casting all your care upon him; for he careth for you" (1 Peter 5:7, KJV).

During your storm, have peace! I call on Jehovah-Nissi, the Lord my Banner, for my God is mighty in battle; I'll yet have peace! After the storm, there is peace, for the Lord my God is my refuge and my fortress, and in Him will I trust. The righteous run unto him and are safe. "He that dwelleth in the secret place of the most High shall abide under the shadow of the Almighty" (Psalms 91:1). There is peace after the storm!

Satan, I rebuke you! Peace when I rise. Peace when I lie down. Peace in my storm. Peace coming out of the storm. I speak peace. You can't have my peace; the stability of my mind depends on it. There WILL be peace beginning, during, and after the storm!

Satan is defeated! I rebuke you in the name of JESUS!

Tekisha D Wimbush

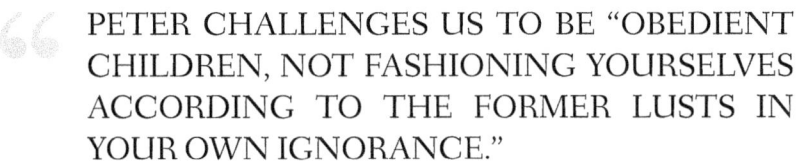

PETER CHALLENGES US TO BE "OBEDIENT CHILDREN, NOT FASHIONING YOURSELVES ACCORDING TO THE FORMER LUSTS IN YOUR OWN IGNORANCE."

"After the storm, there is peace."

Chapter 9
Raise Up Your Standard; There's a Price Tag for the Anointing

Matthew 26:13, Mark 14:3-9, Luke 10:38-42, John 11:17-45;12:1-11

We are talking about Mary, the sister to Lazarus, and Martha, who lived in Bethany. Mary found herself being hospitable to Jesus; she appeared to understand His coming death. Mary gave Him His flowers while He yet lived; she made time for her communion and worship of the Lord, recognizing Him as the Savior.

Mary took care not to be as apprehensive as her sister Martha in the presence of God, Jesus manifested in the Flesh. Mary anointed Him with expensive oil, yet she didn't think twice about the cost. But indignation soon set in with the disciples as they saw her at the feet of Jesus, washing his feet with expensive oil. They felt she could have sold the oil for more than 300 pence ($300 now, then about $45) and the proceeds given to the poor. They began to murmur about her act of worship.

You know there will always be haters. But you ought to tell them, "Don't you criticize my worship," somebody said, "because my worship is for real!" Mary offered all she had from her alabaster box; scripture refers to it as a very precious ointment. Yet she was unconcerned with the profit she could have made. She willingly and unselfishly gave it all to Jesus, who would not always be amongst them.

In life, it is often tempting to settle for mediocrity, the of state or quality of being mediocre—just 'all right,' if you will—even though God said in His word that "Every beast of the forest is mine, and the cattle upon a thousand hills" (Psalms 50:10). Ask what you will of the Father! John 14:12-14 teaches us:

> 12 *Verily, verily, I say unto you, He that believeth on*
> *me, the works that I do shall he do also; and*
> *greater works than these shall he do; because I go*
> *unto my Father.*
> 13 *And whatsoever ye shall ask in my name, that will*
> *I do, that the Father may be glorified in the Son.*
> 14 *If ye shall ask any thing in my name, I will do it.*

All right/okay/mediocre is NOT an option if you believe. You have to raise the bar in your life. Many of us have not done so, though, because we ask not and because we don't believe. Declare, "Mediocrity is not me. That is not of God!"

Remember, this is a faith walk. Hebrews 11:1 challenges us to activate our faith, beginning with the statement:

> *"Now faith is the substance of things hoped for, the*
> *evidence of things not seen."*

You anticipated it was going to happen. You had great certainty and confidence in God, all because of your belief. Have you ever had that feeling in your gut so strong that nothing changed your mind that you could rebuke the enemy with confidence? Because you believed, without a shadow of a doubt, that God would do just what you asked of Him.

In this faith walk with God, there are standards, levels of quality, or attainment. Synonyms: quality, level, grade, caliber, merit, excellence Holiness is a standard. 1st Peter 1:15-16 gives us a definition:

> *15 But as he which hath called you is holy, so be ye*
> *holy in all manner of conversation;*
> *16 Because it is written, Be ye holy; for I am holy.*

Holiness. Being totally submitted to God, set aside for a special use, and set aside from sin and its influence. The 14th verse of 1st Peter challenges us to be "obedient children, not fashioning yourselves according to the former lusts in your own ignorance."

Don't act slow now. Don't you dummy yourself down to refrain from doing the will of the Lord. He is calling us to be holy, for He is Holy. Holiness calls for us to leave those former things behind us. "I don't do that anymore." Whatever that is. Do it for Devine, they said. You should tell the Devil, "No, I ain't gonna do it." When "Why?" is the reaction, should you choose to dignify this question with an explanation in the first place, the way to respond is "Because God said so." He has challenged me to be holy, for He is holy. I choose to worship Him; in my efforts to worship Him, I must be holy. Those who worship Him must worship Him in Spirit and Truth.

I'll raise up my standards in God to be used by him according to His will. "To whom much is given, much is required." There is a price tag for the Anointing.

"Raise up your standard; There is a price tag for the Anointing!" Remind Yourself Daily, "I'm not settling for mediocrity anymore!"

This is all significant. Mediocrity is significant. Holiness is significant. Living in holiness is significant. The significance and complexity of mediocrity and holiness requires me to "Raise my standard" and give God all of me for the Anointing.

I won't settle for "good enough." I am raising up my standard by the power of God in the name of Jesus. "For sin shall not have dominion over you: for ye are not under the law, but under grace" (Romans 6:7). Goodbye, world; you don't mean me no good. Hello, grace; laid up for me is a crown of righteousness. There is a price tag for the Anointing.

> "Jesus paid it all, All to him I owe; Sin has left a
> crimson stain, He washed it white as snow"
>
> — (Elvina Hall, "Jesus Paid It All").

Raise up your standard; There is a price tag for the Anointing. Remember the woman who poured out the oil for Jesus!

_____
_____
_____
_____
_____
_____
_____
_____
_____
_____
_____
_____
_____

_____
_____
_____
_____
_____
_____
_____
_____
_____
_____
_____
_____
_____
_____
_____
_____
_____
_____
_____
_____
_____
_____
_____
_____
_____
_____
_____
_____
_____
_____
_____
_____
_____

PETER CHALLENGES US TO BE "OBEDIENT
CHILDREN, NOT FASHIONING YOURSELVES

ACCORDING TO THE FORMER LUSTS IN YOUR OWN IGNORANCE."

"I'll raise my standards in God."

Chapter 10
I'm not in that place anymore; God has moved me

Apart of human behavior is the ability to change yourself and/or your environment to adapt to your surroundings. This adaptation can occur in one of two ways:

Autoplastic adaptation (alleydog.com) psychology glossary: The subject tries to change himself, i.e., the internal environment.

Alloplastic adaptation (alleydog.com) psychology glossary: The subject tries to change the situation, i.e., the external environment.

I'm not in that place anymore; God has moved me.

Place (n): a particular position or point in space
synonyms: location, site, spot, setting, position, situation, area, region, locale (www.dictionary.com).

Tekisha D Wimbush

Saul to Paul (small in God)

Saul was chosen. We understand from the text of our reading that he was in a certain location/site/setting on the road to Damascus, a commercial city about 175 miles northeast of Jerusalem in the Roman province of Syria.

> Persecute (vt) (dictionary.com): to pursue with harassing or oppressive treatment, especially because of religious or political beliefs, ethnic or racial origin, gender identity, or sexual orientation

Saul was in the position of persecuting the saints of God. Have you ever found yourself in this position of either persecuting or being persecuted for naming the name of the Lord? "Oh, you saved now? You acting funny? You don't go out no more? It don't take all that? You in church all day? Why you go three times a week? What you mean you waiting till you get married? Oh, your Pastor knows everything, huh? Don't judge me. You gave the church all that money? "

I'm not in that place anymore; God has moved me.

Saul found himself in a situation where he was put on the spot, knocked down to his knees, and forced to humble himself in the presence of The Lord. "Saul, Saul, why persecutest thou me?" In this dilemma, Saul replied, but without knowing yet that it was the Lord, he was speaking with. The plot thickens when the Lord reveals himself to Saul: "I am Jesus whom thou persecutest: it is hard for thee to kick against the pricks."

Change is not always easy or comfortable. We often experience that when fighting a positive change. But by resisting a change for the better, you only hurt yourself. In this situation, Saul found himself trembling and astonished, but ultimately he surrendered himself to the Lord: "Lord, what wilt thou have me to do?"

Saul goes on to allow autoplastic change (within himself) to occur in his life. God sent Ananias to Saul, "that you may regain your sight and be filled with the Holy Spirit." Immediately, The Lord removed the scales from his eyes; having regained his sight, he arose and was baptized.

"I'm conscious now; I'm no longer in that place."

As Saul converted to Paul, so have I got my sight; I can see now. Why? Because God has moved me, I'm no longer where I used to be.

Take the stance, "I have been moved to a new dimension in my life with God; He is showing His manifestations to me." I found my resilience;

I bounce back whenever I experience adversity or disappointment. I understand now that the "devil as a roaring lion seeks to devour me," but I'm sober, I'm vigilant, and I got my bearings. He can't have my future because my future is hidden in Christ.

I'm not in that place anymore; God has moved me.

Sister Carol Davis and The Macedonia Mass Choir sang a song, "I moved from my old house / and I moved from my old friends / and I moved from my old way of life / Thank God I moved out / To a brand new life."

"He has created a new spirit within me; He has changed my heart; He has changed my mind." Don't judge me because you can't provoke me; instead of cursing you out or putting my hands on you, I will pray for you. I pray for those who persecute me and those who spitefully use me. Why? Because vengeance is mine, says The Lord. I love those that hate me; I no longer entertain their hate. I no longer drink you under the table. I no longer smoke or use other substances. I no longer take what doesn't belong to me. I am no longer carried away in the lust of my own flesh; instead, I beat this flesh daily, and I beat it under subjection, for sin has no room in my life.

Tekisha D Wimbush

I'm not in that place anymore; God Has moved me.

_____
_____
_____
_____
_____
_____
_____
_____
_____
_____
_____
_____
_____
_____
_____
_____
_____
_____
_____
_____
_____
_____
_____
_____
_____

_____
_____
_____
_____
_____
_____
_____
_____
_____
_____
_____
_____
_____
_____
_____
_____
_____
_____
_____
_____
_____
_____
_____
_____
_____
_____
_____
_____
_____
_____
_____
_____
_____
_____

GOD SHOULD IGNITE SOMETHING IN YOU
TO BRING ABOUT A CHANGE IN YOUR LIFE.

Chapter 11
My God Answers by Fire!

Fire (n) (dictionary.com): a state, process, or instance of combustion in which fuel or other material is ignited and combined with oxygen, giving off light, heat, and flame

Committed (adj) (google.com): feeling dedication and loyalty to a cause, activity, or job; wholeheartedly dedicated
synonyms (thesaurus.com): devoted, faithful, pledged, attached, bound

T he power of God should ignite something in you to bring about a change in your life. Romans 8:28 tells us, "All things work together for good to them that love God, to them who are the called according to his purpose." We know this because God works everything out. Things will not always be good; bad things do happen, even to good people. But God works it out—not just in isolated incidents, but all the time! He works things out for our good. Sometimes it doesn't feel good at first, but it's all for His purpose for those who love Him and trust Him.

God is a God that will not be mocked. His word will not return unto Him void. God says in 1st Chronicles 16:22: "Touch not mine anointed, and do my prophets no harm."

1st Kings 18:1-7, 21-40; 21: 1-16

Key people in this text:

- Ahab, Jezebel, Obadiah
- Elijah the Prophet
- Naboth, owner of the vineyard known as Jezreel
- Other prophets that Jezebel sought to murder
- Children of Israel
- Followers of Baal

Jezebel is recorded to be one of the meanest ladies in the Bible. She made the Israelites suffer to be punished and placed into captivity. Jezebel had convinced Ahab to take Naboth's vineyard—his inheritance from his fathers—by writing false letters that led to the stoning death of Naboth. She taught her servants to worship idols and eat things that were sacrificed unto idols. She also taught them about fornication and adultery, i.e., sexual sins. This ruthless, self-proclaimed "prophetess" failed to repent even when God gave her the space to do so.

According to Revelation 2:20-23, John writes,

> 20 Notwithstanding I have a few things against thee, because thou sufferest that woman Jezebel, which calleth herself a prophetess, to teach and to seduce my servants to commit fornication, and to eat things sacrificed unto idols.
> 21 And I gave her space to repent of her fornication; and she repented not.
> 22 Behold, I will cast her into a bed, and them that

> *commit adultery with her into great tribulation,*
> *except they repent of their deeds.*
> 23 *And I will kill her children with death; and all the*
> *churches shall know that I am he which searcheth*
> *the reins and hearts: and I will give unto every one*
> *of you according to your works.*

Sexual sins hurt God. Why? Because we choose the pleasures of our flesh and do things our way instead of according to God's purpose. We violate our commitment to God, bringing diseases to our bodies, altering our personalities, and destroying our families, churches, and communities because it depletes our integrity. Jezebel was greatly punished for her actions. Her husband, Ahab, was also killed, as well as their son. She died how she lived: Jezebel died a horrible death, having been trampled over and eaten by dogs until nothing remained but her skull, feet, and hands.

My God answers by fire! "Yeah, that just happened!"

Only what you do for Christ will last. God has been proven. In Acts, He declared witnesses unto Him. In Jerusalem, Judea, Samaria, and all the uttermost parts of the earth, the Bible says that the righteous run unto Him, where they are safe.

On the day of Pentecost, God poured out His Spirit as fire. There appeared cloven tongues, and they all began to speak with other tongues as the Spirit gave them this utterance.

Paul writes to the church at Thessalonica and believers everywhere (1 Thessalonians 5:23):

> 23 *And the very God of peace sanctify you wholly;*
> *and I pray God your whole spirit and soul and*
> *body be preserved blameless unto the coming of*
> *our Lord Jesus Christ.*

God must be involved in every aspect of our lives. We cannot separate our spiritual lives from everything else - one body, one faith.

In 1st Timothy 4:8-9, Paul writes to Timothy, a young leader of the early Christian community:

> 8 *For bodily exercise profiteth little: but godliness is profitable unto all things, having promise of the life that now is, and of that which is to come.*

It's an acceptance that by faith, I use the abilities God has given me in the service of His church.

Romans 12:1-21, KJV

> 12 *I beseech you therefore, brethren, by the mercies of God, that ye present your bodies a living sacrifice, holy, acceptable unto God, which is your reasonable service.*
> 2 *And be not conformed to this world: but be ye transformed by the renewing of your mind, that ye may prove what is that good, and acceptable, and perfect, will of God.*

_____
_____
_____
_____
_____
_____
_____
_____
_____
_____

HE HEALETH THE BROKEN IN HEART, AND BINDETH UP THEIR WOUNDS.

"My God answers by fire!"

Chapter 12
Are You Spiritually and Naturally Fit? Allow Me to Heal

Heal (vt) (dictionary.com): (1) To make healthy, whole, or sound; restore to health; free from ailment. (2) to bring to an end or conclusion, as conflicts between people or groups, usually with the strong implication of restoring former amity; settle; reconcile. (3) to free from evil; cleanse; purify

I've been wounded, hurt, let down, disappointed, misunderstood, lied to, cheated, talked about behind my back, mistreated, used, mentally and physically abused, confused, accused, scorned, oppressed, depressed, in distress, in a mess. But allow me to heal!

> 4 Surely he hath borne our griefs, and carried our
>   sorrows: yet we did esteem him stricken, smitten of
>   God, and afflicted.
> 5 But he was wounded for our transgressions, he was
>   bruised for our iniquities: the chastisement of our
>   peace was upon him; and with his stripes we are
>   healed.

— (Isaiah 53:4-5)

We take comfort in the healing words of Psalms 147:3 :

> 3 *He healeth the broken in heart, and bindeth up their wounds.*

Are you spiritually and naturally fit? Allow me to heal.

> proverb (n) (dictionary.com): A profound saying, maxim, or oracular utterance requiring interpretation

Proverbs are short poems, usually in couplet form, containing a holy mixture of common sense and timely warnings. It gives us advice that will help us to walk closely with God! The word "proverb" comes from a Hebrew word which means "to rule or to govern."

> 5 *Let this mind be in you, which was also in Christ Jesus*

— (Philippians 2:5)

The Bible's book of Proverbs is a collection of wise yet practical suggestions for effectively living our daily lives in God.

> *"The fear of The Lord is the beginning of knowledge: but fools despise wisdom and instruction."*

— (Proverbs 1:7)

Solomon, the author of the book of Proverbs, was the world's wisest man at his time. He wanted to impart wisdom to all of mankind even as he pursued wisdom from God! (e.g., 1 Kings 3:5-14)

_____

_____

_____

_____

_____

_____

_____

_____

_____

_____

_____

_____

_____

_____

_____

_____

_____

_____

_____

_____

_____

_____

_____

_____

_____

_____

_____

_____

_____

 THE WISE PERSON PURSUES KNOWLEDGE AND LOVE OF GOD. WISDOM WILL KEEP ME FROM DISASTER!

Tekisha D Wimbush

"Allow me to heal."

Chapter 13
In Pursuit of My Happiness

Have you encountered an individual in your life who gave good advice on resolving a dilemma? I mean, advice that you could hear, see, and feel, to the point that you used their advice and found yourself at their mercy as you repeatedly sought their advice? With the understanding that their own life was also a complete mess, yet they gave you such good advice that you felt and believed? Not even for certain that they had your best interest at heart? But it sounded good; it felt good at the moment.

We must understand that "knowledge" (having facts) and "wisdom" (applying those facts to life) are two different things. Without wisdom, knowledge is ineffective. We must learn how to live out loud, live out what we know.

The Pursuit of Happiness: 07/07/1776
pursue (vt) (dictionary.com): To strive to gain; seek to attain or accomplish (an end, object, purpose, etc.)

"Life, Liberty, and the pursuit of Happiness" is a well-known phrase in the United States Declaration of Independence. The phrase gives examples of the various "unalienable rights" which the Declaration says all human beings have been provided by their Creator, and for the protection of which they institute governments. What's unalienable cannot be taken away, denied, surrendered, sold, or transferred to someone else.

The wise person pursues knowledge and love of God. Wisdom will keep me from disaster! Wisdom will keep me from being reckless! Wisdom will save me from myself!

I have a "right" to be happy. I have a right to "pursue" what makes me "happy"! For God has made me glad!

"I'm in pursuit of my happiness"! – "There are benefits of seeking Godly wisdom!"

In my pursuit, I have found that a close relationship with God makes me Happy. He gives me joy and peace through wisdom, knowledge, and understanding. In times of storms and adversity, He gives me the wisdom to endure hard trials.

 GOD HAS CHOSEN US. WE ARE NOT SAVED
BECAUSE WE DESERVE IT, BUT BECAUSE OF

THE GRACE OF GOD

"I have a right to be happy."

Chapter 14
Because God has left His Imprint upon Me

I Am a Seed of the Promise; Imprint on Me, O Lord

In Ephesians 1:4-6, Paul wrote to the church in Ephesus, his last trip that he would take there. The purpose of the letter was to strengthen the Ephesian believers in their Christian faith by explaining the nature and purpose of the church, the body of Christ.

> 4 According as he hath chosen us in him before the
>   foundation of the world, that we should be holy
>   and without blame before him in love:
> 5 Having predestinated us unto the adoption of
>   children by Jesus Christ to himself, according to
>   the good pleasure of his will,
> 6 To the praise of the glory of his grace, wherein he
>   hath made us accepted in the beloved.

imprint (vt) (lexico.com): (1) impress or stamp (a mark or outline) on a surface. (2) make an impression or mark on. (3) fix (an idea) firmly in someone's mind.

God had already imprinted upon us. He had already left a mark upon His chosen generation. I was chosen before the foundation of the world. I am a seed of the promise!

In Genesis 12:1-3, God promised Abraham to make his name great, although not without sacrifice. With unwavering belief, he obeyed God, left his family and his kindred behind, and went to the place God sent him. Only then could he become the father of a great nation. Only then could he receive the Promise. God then said that "I will bless them that bless thee, and curse them that curseth thee: and in thee shall all families of the earth be blessed" (Genesis 12:3).

I am a seed of the Promise. Imprint.

Paul tells us in Ephesians 1:4 that God has chosen us. We are not saved because we deserve it but because of the grace of God, Who freely gives It.

Paul states that it was "predestined," marked out beforehand. God adopted us as His own children through the sacrifice of Jesus Christ. There is atonement. Paul reminds us of the mark that God's imprint left upon us.

I was all in God's plan! (1 Timothy 3:16):

> 16 And without controversy great is the mystery of
> godliness: God was manifest in the flesh, justified
> in the Spirit, seen of angels, preached unto the
> Gentiles, believed on in the world, received up
> into glory.

You are a mark because God has left His imprint upon you! I am a seed of the Promise. Imprint.

According to Romans 8:16-17, God made me a joint heir with Christ through the lineage of David. God chose me. Thank God for His imprint!

16 ...we are the children of God:

17 And if children, then heirs; heirs of God, and joint-heirs with Christ; if so be that we suffer with him, that we may also be glorified together.

But only after you suffer will you behold the glory of the Lord—yes, after heartache, depression, persecution, being lied to, etc.

Psalm 27:4 tells us: "One thing have I desired of the Lord, that will I seek after; that I may dwell in the house of the Lord all the days of my life, to behold the beauty of the Lord, and to enquire in his temple."

All because He imprinted on ME!

I am a seed of the Promise. Imprint. Render unto God what belongs to Him. All souls belong to God!

_____
_____
_____
_____
_____
_____
_____
_____
_____
_____
_____
_____
_____
_____
_____
_____
_____
_____
_____

Tekisha D Wimbush

_____
_____
_____
_____
_____
_____
_____
_____
_____
_____
_____
_____
_____
_____
_____
_____
_____
_____
_____
_____
_____
_____
_____
_____
_____

 WE DEVELOP THE SPIRITUAL FITNESS AND
DISCIPLINE WE NEED TO PUSH PAST OUR
LIFE CIRCUMSTANCES AND PROBLEMS.

"I was all in God's plan."

Chapter 15
It's Time To Make A Change

Purpose (n) (dictionary.com): the reason for which something exists or is done, made, used, etc. (v): to intend; design

King Solomon wrote the book of Ecclesiastes to an audience of people in general. He wanted everyone to understand that life experiences apart from God are meaningless and that there is a right time for everything. God has a plan for each of our lives; all things happen in God's time.

Scripture says,

> *"And we know that all things work together for good to them that love God, to them who are the called according to his purpose."*

> — (Romans 8:28)

This is for those who love and accept God and live according to His purpose. Not to those fulfilling the lust of the flesh nor conforming to the things of this world. Christians are to be Christ-like. It's time to be purposeful with our walk in our freedom. It's time that we stand up and be counted! Paul charged us to "Stand fast therefore in the liberty wherewith Christ hath made us free, and be not again entangled with the yoke of bondage" (Galatians 5:1). I won't go back!

In Hebrews 12:1-2, Paul charged us to "lay aside every weight, and the sin which doth so easily beset us, and let us run with patience the race that is set before us." He challenges us to turn our minds and focus on Jesus, "the author and finisher of our faith." We develop spiritual fitness and discipline through Him to push past our life circumstances and problems.

It's time to make a change!

> Romans 12:2: *"And be not conformed to this world: but be ye transformed by the renewing of your mind, that ye may prove that what is that good, and acceptable, and perfect will of God."*
> 2 Corinthians 5:17: *"Therefore if any man be in Christ, he is a new creature: old things are passed away; behold all things are become new."*

Now, although change is good, it's not always comfortable. To start anew, you must give up your old ways for God's. Sacrifices are key to a closer relationship with God.

Forget the former things; I'm leaving that baggage behind me. Let's go to the potter's house instead! (Jeremiah 18:1-6). God is the potter, and I am the clay. Lord, make me over; Make A Change.

_____
_____
_____
_____
_____
_____
_____
_____
_____
_____
_____
_____
_____
_____
_____
_____
_____
_____
_____
_____
_____
_____
_____
_____
_____
_____
_____
_____
_____
_____
_____

WE DEVELOP THE SPIRITUAL FITNESS AND
DISCIPLINE WE NEED TO PUSH PAST OUR
LIFE CIRCUMSTANCES AND PROBLEMS.

Tekisha D Wimbush

"God is the potter, and I am the clay."

Chapter 16
Off The Grid

But why, when God has given us the path to salvation and eternal life

Psalms 118:29: "O give thanks unto The Lord; for he
is good: for his mercy endureth for ever."

Psalms 119:105: "Thy word is a lamp unto my feet,
and a light unto my path."

Psalms 119:11: "Thy word have I hid in mine heart,
that I might not sin against thee."

2 Timothy 3:16: "All scripture is given by inspiration
of God, and is profitable for doctrine, for reproof,
for correction, for instruction in righteousness."

You may recall from an earlier chapter our discussion of the Bible as our basic instructions before leaving earth. God delivered unto the

Israelites His law, containing hundreds of specific commands that flow out of the ten commandments. But the phrase "the law" refers specifically to the compilation of decrees found in the first five books of the Bible, known in the Jewish faith as the Torah.

This repetitive meditation focuses on the beauty of God's word, which inclines us toward purity and helps us grow in the Lord and faith.

The 22 sections of Psalms 119 were written with the Hebrew alphabet, and each verse begins with the letter of its section. Because many Hebrews did not have personal copies of the scriptures to read as we do, the repetitive structure of the scriptures helped them memorize them and pass them along orally.

Repeat Psalms 118:29:

> "O give thanks unto the Lord; for he is good: for his
> mercy endureth forever."

God knew and understood that for man to keep His commandments, man must know His commandments. This is what the psalmist meant in Psalms 119:11. The bible will not always be with us. This is why we must not go "off the grid"; God has given us the path to salvation and eternal life!

Romans 10:9 tells us: "That if thou shalt confess with thy mouth the Lord Jesus, and shalt believe in thine heart that God hath raised him from the dead, thou shalt be saved." We must also understand that memorization without the scripture's application profits nothing. We must apply the scriptures to our daily lives and activate the power that God has given us according to Acts:1:8:

> "But ye shall receive power, after that the Holy Ghost
> is come upon you: and ye shall be witnesses unto
> me both in Jerusalem, and in all Judaea, and in

Samaria, and unto the uttermost part of the earth."

Question, "Why are you 'off the grid' when God has given us the path to salvation and eternal life?" As God's new creation, we are made to obey His law, not because it gets us anything but because of our love for Him. We must take on the attitude portrayed by Jesus, as spoken by the Psalmist (i.e., David) in his ageless words: "I delight to do thy will, O my God; yea, thy law is within my heart" (Psalm 40:8).

If you're "off the grid" today, I ask that you get back on. Guide me, Jesus. "Therefore if any man be in Christ, he is a new creature: old things are passed away; behold, all things become new" (2 Corinthians 5:17).

_____
_____
_____
_____
_____
_____
_____
_____
_____
_____
_____
_____
_____
_____
_____
_____
_____

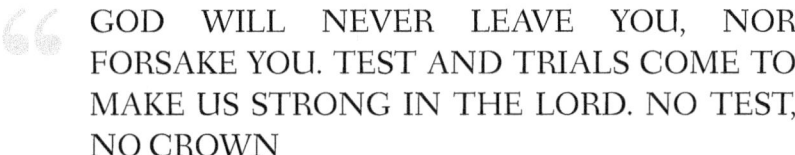 GOD WILL NEVER LEAVE YOU, NOR FORSAKE YOU. TEST AND TRIALS COME TO MAKE US STRONG IN THE LORD. NO TEST, NO CROWN

"We must apply scripture to our daily lives."

Chapter 17
Out of the Belly of the Beast

Jonah 2:1-10

The book of the prophet Jonah was written by Jonah, son of Amittai. Its purpose is to show the extent of God's grace and that the message of salvation is for all people.

Jonah was to go to Nineveh, the capital of the Assyrian nation, to declare that they must repent from their wicked ways (of evil plots against God, exploitation of the helpless, cruelty in war, idolatry, prostitution, witchcraft, etc.).

Jonah hated the Assyrian people; he knew that if they repented, God would forgive them and not destroy them. This led Jonah to abort God's mission for him. Jonah's biases prevented him from understanding that the Gospel is for all who will repent. God is to be shared, not kept to ourselves. The Bible says, "Go ye therefore, and teach all nations" (Matthew 28:19).

Who are we to judge someone else? Who are we to decide whom God should or should not forgive?

We often find ourselves defiant when it comes to obeying God. We often turn and go in the opposite direction He is leading us. Deviating from God's plan for us brings only damnation to ourselves and grief to the ones we love.

Ask yourself, "Has God asked you to do something you have not done"?

Although we fail to adhere to God's requests, God, in His mercy, sees fit to give us another chance when we return unto Him. We should not run from God but trust Him with our past, present, and future. It is better to obey God in the first place than to suffer the dire consequences of going our own way. Disobedience to God stirs Him to anger, endangering ourselves and others, especially those close to us.

Those who say they love God cannot also run from Him at the same time. Understanding that you cannot run from God is critical to pleasing Him. To gain more power from Him, you must draw nigh to Him and obey Him by doing what He says. We cannot be merely hearers of the word; we must also be doers of the word.

Jonah was not of this conviction initially while he was running from God. Because he was obedient to his own emotions, he failed to line up with God's spirit. In times like these, we fail to understand that we are essentially worshipping idols!

> *"Thou shall have none other gods before me."*
>
> — (Deuteronomy 5:7).

Idols don't have to be just physical objects; anything that we put in front of God, anything that causes us to disobey God's word and His commandments, can be an idol.

Therefore, we must put God at the head of our lives. In any situation, our perspective must be to put God first (e.g., God, husband, children). It is human to struggle with this as we place our loved ones, jobs, children, and spouses ahead of God. But in doing so, we put ourselves at risk of suffering His wrath.

Yet through repentance, there is still hope for us! Repentance is for everyone; it requires you to be Godly, sorrowful of your wicked ways of sin, and turn yourself back toward God. Peter said in Acts 2:38:

> *"Repent, and be baptized every one of you in the name of Jesus Christ for the remission of sins, and ye shall receive the gift of the Holy Ghost."*

God is a God of forgiveness—but only if we repent and ask sincerely for forgiveness, and then sin no more. Jonah found himself in the belly of a whale for three days and three nights. God sure got his attention! What will it take for him to get yours?

Are you in the belly of a beast in your life right now? Do you have baggage that won't cut you loose? Are you being tossed about with troubles in your life? Well, are you failing to obey God and keep His commandments? Woe unto thee!

God is calling for sincere repentance. Yeah, Lord! Out of the belly of the beast!

Jonah thanked God right in the belly of the beast; in the midst of his dilemma and his self-inflicted crisis, he began to thank God and to pray unto Him. That is what finally led to his deliverance.

Even in the midst of God breaking him down, he humbled himself and looked to the holy temple of God. The word comes not to tear you down, but to build you up; not to have you run from God, but to draw nigh to Him. He didn't just pray for deliverance as we do when we get in trouble.

We must always maintain a close relationship with God, including good times, to ensure balance.

Jonah cried from the belly of hell for his deliverance, and God heard his cry. You have to want to be delivered, and then you have to fight to hold on to your deliverance. "Nay, we are more than conquerors through him that loved us" (Romans 8:37). Sometimes, we have to seek God's strength to navigate through this spiritual warfare: "He maketh my feet like hinds' feet, and setteth me upon high places" (Psalms 18:33). And that's okay! God will never leave you nor forsake you. Tests and trials come to make us strong in the Lord. No test, No crown.

Out of the belly of the beast! Whatever the beast may BE.

_____

_____

_____

_____

_____

_____

_____

_____

_____

_____

_____

_____

_____

_____

_____

_____

_____

_____
_____
_____
_____
_____
_____
_____
_____
_____
_____
_____
_____
_____
_____
_____
_____
_____
_____
_____
_____
_____
_____
_____
_____
_____
_____
_____
_____
_____
_____
_____
_____
_____
_____
_____
_____
_____
_____
_____

 GOD COMMANDS US TO SEEK HIS WISDOM
REGARDING THE DIRECTION HE WOULD

HAVE US GO

"Those who say they love God cannot run from him at the same time."

Chapter 18
Let Our Devotion Be Pleasing to God As we Seek Him

Psalms 19:12-14

12 *Who can understand his errors? cleanse thou me from secret faults.*

13 *Keep back thy servant also from presumptuous sins; let them not have dominion over me: then shall I be upright, and I shall be innocent from the great transgression.*

14 *Let the words of my mouth, and the mediation of my heart, be acceptable in thy sight, O LORD, my strength, and my redeemer.*

In this psalm, David's knowledge of God inspires him to deepen his devotion to his Lord. He wants to rid his life of both willful sins and hidden faults. David ends the psalm with a prayer that his words and inner thoughts would be pleasing to God, whom he acknowledges as his strength and redeemer.

1 Thessalonians 4:3-5 and 5:16-18 give specific examples of behavior clearly aligned with God's will.

> 3 *For this is the will of God, even your sanctification,*
>   *that ye should abstain from fornication:*
> 4 *That every one of you should know how to possess*
>   *his vessel in sanctification and honour;*
> 5 *Not in the lust of concupiscence, even as the*
>   *Gentiles which know not God."*

> 16 *Rejoice evermore.*
> 17 *Pray without ceasing.*
> 18 *In everything give thanks: for this is the will of God*
>   *in Christ Jesus concerning you."*

We know that God's will is not always clear to us. In these instances, God commands us to seek His wisdom regarding the direction He would have us go. Proverbs 3:5-6 says,

> "5 *Trust in the LORD with all thine heart; and lean*
>   *not unto thine own understanding.*
> 6 *In all thy ways acknowledge him, and he shall direct*
>   *thy paths."*

John 14:13-15 writes,

> "13 *And whatsoever ye shall ask in my name, that will*
>   *I do, that the Father may be glorified in the Son.*
> 14 *If ye shall ask anything in my name, I will do it.*
> 15 *If ye love me, keep my commandments."*

It is God's will and desire for us to prosper in Him!

> *"Beloved, I wish above all things that thou mayest prosper and be in health, even as thy soul prospereth."*
>
> — (3 John 1:2)

God desires that we know His will and plan for our lives. As we earnestly seek Him, we find truth:

> *"Having made known unto us the mystery of his will, according to his good pleasure which he hath purposed in himself."*
>
> — (Ephesians 1:9)

_____
_____
_____
_____
_____
_____
_____
_____
_____
_____
_____
_____
_____
_____
_____
_____
_____

Tekisha D Wimbush

IN OUR STRUGGLE WITH SIN, WE NEED SPIRITUAL PERSISTENCE.

"As we earnestly seek Him, we find truth."

Chapter 19
I Came to Bless Him

Genesis 32:24-30

Sometimes in life, you must fight for what you want. You must be determined in your struggle with whomever or whatever is opposing you. The struggle is worth it, though, for struggling under tough conditions builds strong character. In our struggle with sin, we need spiritual persistence.

Jacob and Esau, the twin sons of Isaac, struggled even while in the womb. Jacob held his brother's heel at birth and later stole his brother's birthright and their father Isaac's final blessing with it. But God would soon change his life, just as he did with Saul/Paul on the road to Damascus.

Jacob wrestled all night to the break of dawn to be blessed by God. He was persistent while in pursuit, even suffering an injury to his thigh. "How bad do you want it?" Up to that moment, Jacob was known as an ambitious deceiver. But one night, because he struggled with God and prevailed, he received a new name, Israel, and a new purpose. I won't Let go till You bless me!

Even in the midst of adversity, one must bless the Lord and make known His good deeds. David said,

> 1 I will bless the LORD at all times: his praise shall continually be in my mouth.
> 2 My soul shall make her boast in the LORD: the humble shall hear thereof, and be glad.
> 3 O magnify the LORD with me, and let us exalt his name together.
>
> — (Psalms 24:1-3)

I came to bless Him! God has great blessings for His people. But many of these blessings require our active participation!

Let us require ourselves to have faith in God. Refrain from sin; turn from our wicked ways; draw nigh to God; seek His face. Be separate from the world. Have spiritual tunnel vision and lock in on the prize!

I came to bless Him!

In the midst of my dilemmas, trials, and tribulations, I will bless the Lord. In the midst of my disappointments. "I will say of the Lord, He is my refuge and my fortress: my God; in him will I trust." (Psalms 91:2). When it seems like the odds are stacked against me, I will bless Him. "Who shall separate us from the love of Christ? shall tribulation, or distress, or persecution, or famine, or nakedness, or peril, or sword?" (Romans 8:35). Paul goes on to say that nothing shall separate us from the love of God, which is in Christ Jesus our Lord. I will be like Jacob and hold on to God. I won't let go until you bless me, Lord.

I came to bless Him! I will bless Him in my good days as well as my bad days. I will shout with a voice of triumph, for He inhabits the praises of His people.

I came to bless Him!

_____

_____

_____

_____

_____

_____

_____

_____

_____

_____

_____

_____

_____

_____

_____

_____

_____

_____

_____

_____

_____

_____

_____

_____

_____

_____

_____

_____

_____

_____
_____
_____
_____
_____
_____
_____
_____
_____
_____
_____
_____
_____
_____
_____
_____
_____
_____
_____
_____
_____
_____
_____
_____
_____
_____

 I SPEAK LIFE! COME FORTH OUT OF YOUR
DEAD SITUATION! IN THE MIDST OF

DOUBTING SPECTATORS, OF UNBELIEVERS, OF HATERS, OF PERSECUTORS, I SPEAK LIFE!

"Nothing shall separate us from the love of God."

Chapter 20
I Speak Life

Proverbs 18:21: "Death and life are in the power of the tongue: and they that love it shall eat the fruit thereof."

No matter my condition, I am speaking my disposition!

disposition (n) (dictionary.com): the predominant or prevailing tendency of one's spirits; natural mental and emotional outlook or mood; characteristic attitude

condition (n) (dictionary.com): a particular mode of being of a person or thing; existing state; situation with respect to circumstances

In James 5:13-18, James asked about the conditions of the people. "Is any among you afflicted [the condition of being sick]?" His response was to do something about it: "Let him pray." Change your disposition: "Is any merry [the condition of being cheerful]?" Do something: "Let them sing psalms." "Is any sick among you?" etc.

But all sickness is not unto death: " 14 Let him call for the elders of the church, and let them pray over him, anointing him with oil in the name of the Lord: 15 And the prayer of faith shall save the sick, and the Lord shall raise him up; and if he have committed sins, they shall be forgiven him."

Speaking life means that one must open their mouth and utter words that are effectual and fervent out of it.

> effectual (adj) (dictionary.com): producing or capable of producing an intended effect; adequate

> fervent (adj) (dictionary.com): having or showing great warmth or intensity of spirit, feeling, enthusiasm, etc.; ardent

We, therefore, understand the scripture when James says in 5:16, "Confess your faults one to another, and pray one for another, that ye may be healed. The effectual fervent prayer of a righteous man availeth much." Therefore, let us speak life and not death to circumstances requiring life. We must speak positive affirmations that generate life to our conditions, circumstances, or situations.

James, brother of Jesus and a leader in Jerusalem, is speaking to first-century Christians everywhere in an effort to expose unethical practices and to teach the right steps toward righteousness: James 1:21 "Wherefore lay apart all filthiness and superfluity of naughtiness, and receive with meekness the engrafted word, which is able to save your souls" (James 1:21).

Speaking life requires action too, though: "But be ye doers of the word, and not hearers only, deceiving your own selves" (James 1:22). Are we speaking the word AND doing the word so that it may be manifested fully in our lives? The author of Psalms—the longest book of the Bible, some attribute to David and others to Ezra—expresses in

119:11 a personal affirmation: "Thy word I have hid in mine heart, that I might not sin against thee." James refers to this as the Engrafted Word. For "in the beginning was the Word, and the Word was with God, and the Word was God" (John 1:1). For, in the beginning, God moved upon the face of the deep, upon the waters, even right in the midst of death and darkness, to speak life: "And God said, Let there be light: and there was light."

(Genesis 1:3). If you need light in your life in your dark situation, speak light in the name of Jesus! If you need deliverance in your life, speak! I am delivered! I am set free! Ain't no chains holding me! I speak life; in the midst of my condition, I'm speaking my disposition. I speak life!

Speak life into existence; speak it before you see it.

"Lazarus, come forth" (John 11:43). In the midst of a dead situation, in the condition of decomposition after four days, Jesus called on Lazarus to return to life. I speak life! Come forth out of your dead situation! In the midst of doubting spectators, of unbelievers, of haters, of persecutors, I speak life! Whose report shall you believe? I believe the report of the Lord.

Part of being a doer of the word is for our disposition to be based upon factual evidence. We must understand James's plight of being purged and cleansed from all wickedness so that we may come to the Lord and commune with Him in "effectual prayer." We petition God through Jesus Christ so that we may speak to those things that are not as they seem. That we may speak life even in the midst of death and deadly conditions. That we change our dispositions, freeing ourselves to speak life in the first place. That the perfect will of God be manifested in our lives with validated outcomes—thus allowing me to testify to the goodness of Jesus. Lord, grant me the ability to say, "won't God do it"!

Tekisha D Wimbush

What is your "Personal Affirmation"? "Death and life are in the power of the tongue: and they that love it shall eat the fruit thereof " (Proverbs 18:21).

In the condition of darkness at a time in Israel's history, there were no kings. "In those days there was no king in Israel, but every man did that which was right in his own eyes" (Judges 17:6). People lived to please themselves. But God! Following Judges is the book of Ruth, whose authorship is unknown (although often attributed to Samuel, the author of Judges). The author's purpose in writing Ruth, which is set after the period of the judges, was to show three particular people —Ruth, Naomi, and Boaz—ways to remain strong in character and true to God even when the society around them was collapsing. When history repeats itself, will you speak life? Will you remain true to God?

Although both were in the condition of being widows, Ruth spoke her own affirmation to Naomi about remaining in God, inspiring Naomi to change her own disposition: "And Ruth said, Intreat me not to leave thee, or to return from following after thee: for wither thou goest, I will go; and where thou lodgest, I will lodge: thy people shall be my people, and thy God my God" (Ruth 1:16). Ruth's affirmation and choice to speak life in God led her to her new husband, Boaz. But more significantly, it led her to give birth to Obed, father of Jesse, father of David—out of whose lineage came our savior, Jesus Christ!

Are you speaking and living this life to live again in heaven with the Lord? Are you speaking and overcoming the sins of this world? Are you stepping out into the joy of the Lord? Is the joy of the Lord your strength? Are you speaking life to your own life circumstances? Are you speaking that I'm more than a Conqueror? I'm Victorious!; I'm above, and not beneath! Are you speaking that Satan is defeated and God is victorious? Shall you live and not die?

Are you changing your disposition in the midst of your condition? Are you speaking life?

I speak life, and I'm living my life more abundantly, for greater is he that is within Me—the Engrafted Word, the Holy Ghost, the comforter—than he that is in the world. I speak life no matter my condition! I'm speaking my disposition through the power of the Holy Ghost. In the mighty name of Jesus, my faith has He made me whole. It is God who gives the increase; increase in me, O God. Create a new and a right spirit within me. I speak life to my business; I speak life to my church home.

I speak life!

_____
_____
_____
_____
_____
_____
_____
_____
_____
_____
_____
_____
_____
_____
_____
_____
_____
_____
_____
_____
_____
_____

_____
_____
_____
_____
_____
_____
_____
_____
_____
_____
_____
_____
_____
_____
_____
_____
_____
_____
_____
_____
_____
_____
_____
_____

> WE NEED TO EMULATE GODLY CHARACTERISTICS, IN RELATION TO THE FRUITS OF THE SPIRIT: LOVE, JOY, PEACE, PATIENCE, KINDNESS, GOODNESS, FAITHFULNESS, AND IN SELF-CONTROL.

"Speak life into existence."

Chapter 21
I Am Built for This

oses is credited as the author of the book of Genesis. He is the one to whom God revealed Himself as the I AM, who sent Moses to deliver His people from bondage (Exodus 3:14). Moses wrote the book for the children of Israel to record God's creation of the world and His desire to have a people set apart to worship Him: "And God said, Let us make man in our image, after our likeness: and let them have dominion over the fish of the sea, and over the fowl of the air, and over the cattle, and over all the earth, and over every creeping thing that creepeth upon the earth" (Genesis 1:26). God was very pleased with the creation work He had finished by the end of the sixth day:

> "And God saw everything that he had made, and,
> behold, it was very good. And the evening and the
> morning were the sixth day."

> — (Genesis 1:31)

Thanks to the revelation of I AM to man; we have a direct representation of who God is and who we are to Him. That is why I have the courage to say: I am built for this!

When you understand that we were created in the image of God, you understand that we need to emulate Godly characteristics in relation to the fruits of the spirit: love, joy, peace, patience, kindness, goodness, faithfulness, and self-control. Knowing that you are created in the image of God and that you share His characteristics provides a solid foundation of Christian self-worth. Worldly possessions, achievements, physical attractiveness, or public acclaim do not define our understanding of human worth. Rather, it is about being made in the image of God. You are a person of infinite worth. We can feel positive about ourselves; we have the freedom to love God and the ability to know Him and have a personal relationship with Him:

> 13 *For thou hast possessed my reins: thou hast covered*
> *me in my mother's womb.*
> 14 *I will praise thee; for I am fearfully and*
> *wonderfully made: marvelous are thy works; and*
> *that my soul knoweth right well.*
> 15 *My substance was not hid from thee, when I was*
> *made in secret, and curiously wrought in the*
> *lowest parts of the earth.*
>
> — (Psalms 139:13-15)

I am built for this!

Though tests and trials may come, I understand that no weapon formed against me shall prevail. I am a conqueror! God's character goes into the creation of every person—even when feeling worthless, depressed, oppressed, rejected, dejected, lied to, cheated, persecuted, gossiped about, abused, scorned, degraded, broken, hated, or unforgiven. Remember, "22 But the fruit of the Spirit is love joy, peace, longsuffering, gentleness, goodness, faith, 23 Meekness, temperance: against such there is no law" (Galatians 5:22-23). Whether I'm up or down, I won't give up in the spirit, for I am built with the fruit of the indwelling Spirit of the Holy Ghost. Old things are passed away; behold, I am a new creation in Christ!

I Am Built for This!

_____

_____

_____

_____

_____

_____

_____

_____

_____

_____

_____

_____

_____

_____

_____

_____

_____

_____

_____

_____

_____

Tekisha D Wimbush

AS THE SAYING GOES, "FAVOR AIN'T FAIR, BUT IT'S RIGHT."

"You are a person of infinite worth."

Chapter 22
Favor after Failure

Judges 16:6

failure (n) (dictionary.com): 1. an act or instance of failing or proving unsuccessful; lack of success; 2. nonperformance of something due, required, or expected

favor (n) (dictionary.com): the state of being approved or held in regard

When we look at failure, we think about the non-completion of some task we wanted to do or the non-achievement of some goal or objective we set for ourselves. Consider what Proverbs has to say about marriage:

"Whoso findeth a wife findeth a good thing, and obtaineth favour of the LORD."

— (Proverbs 18:22)

God created marriage as a joyful and good institution. He pronounced marriage to be good and honorable in His sight. As we downplay and exploit marriage, though—as we lie in the presence of the Lord and bear false witness in church and to the clergy and witnesses we invited— we see that marriage failures are on the rise.

We all know that many see partiality of favor in our finite sight, often wondering how that could happen for them when in fact, they are living contrary to what God has declared. As the saying goes, "Favor ain't fair, but it's right." But what if we say this instead: God is fair and above human partiality. God's favor is right. We all know that God has shown us favor in our failures and our self-inflicted nonsense. God blesses us with His favor. Nod your head if you know this to be true!

Right in the midst of Israel being delivered into the hands of the Philistines for 40 years, favor was shown to Manoah and his wife, who was barren and had no children. God revealed to Manoah's wife by an angel that she would conceive a son. However, she was told to drink no wine nor strong drink, eat no unclean thing and have no razor come upon his head. For this unborn child was to be consecrated as a Nazarite unto God, for he would begin the delivery of Israel out of the hands of the Philistines. Samson served as a judge for 20 years, in the time before Israel had kings.

> "In those days, there was no king in Israel, but every
> man did that which was right in his own eyes."
>
> — (Judges 17:6)

Samson, who was blessed with great physical strength, was part of God's plan. Samson had desired to marry a Philistine even though they were the oppressors. Having been tricked at his own wedding feast, he went to Ashkelton, where he killed some Philistines and took their coats to settle a bet he had lost. Samson then allowed himself to be captured and brought to Lehigh, where he called upon the Lord's strength once more to avenge the Philistines, who had blinded him:

> 28 *And Samson called unto the LORD, and said, O Lord GOD, remember me, I pray thee, and strengthen me, I pray thee, only this once, O God, that I may be at once avenged of the Philistines for my two eyes.*
> 29 *And Samson took hold of the two middle pillars upon which the house stood, and on which it was borne up, of the one with his right hand, and of the other with his left.*
> 30 *And Samson said, Let me die with the Philistines. And he bowed himself with all his might; and the house fell upon the lords, and upon all the people that were therein. So the dead which he slew at his death were more than they which he slew in his life.*
>
> — (Judges 16:28-30)

Samson apparently received the favor he requested, although, for some, failure could be pondered. Contrary to God, there is no failure seems Samson completed his work. What are your thoughts as you read the story?

_____
_____
_____
_____
_____

_____

_____

_____

_____

_____

_____

_____

_____

_____

_____

_____

_____

_____

_____

_____

_____

_____

_____

_____

_____

_____

_____

_____

_____

_____

_____

" DON'T COMPLAIN ABOUT WHAT YOU
DON'T HAVE, DON'T WORRY ABOUT

THINGS YOU DON'T SEE IN THE NATURAL WORLD, DON'T LET WORRY DROWN OUT YOUR PRAYER LIFE.

"God blesses us with His favor."

Chapter 23
I have the More— But only if I Believe

"He that believes on him shall not perish but have everlasting life."

— Genesis 12:1-5

more (adj) (dictionary.com): in greater quantity, amount, measure, degree, or number

dominion (n) (dictionary.com): 1. the power or right of governing and controlling; sovereign authority; 2. rule; control; domination

Genesis 1: 26-29: In the beginning, God created man in His own image and after His own likeness. He declared that man shall have dominion over all the earth: the fish of the sea, the fowl of the air, the cattle, the creeping things upon the earth. He goes on to create male and female in His own image, and then to bless them, saying in verse 28: "Be fruitful, and multiply, and replenish the earth and subdue it." In verse 29, God goes further in describing the more he gave to mankind: "Behold, I have given you every herb bearing seed, which is upon the face of all the earth, and every tree, in the which is the fruit of a tree yielding seed; to you it shall be for meat."

Even though mankind had the more, they still managed to succumb to Satan's temptations. Forsaking their faith in God, they yielded to unbelief and catered to their own selfish desires. Why do this when all this time God always gives us the more? After all, He made us and not we ourselves. Following the fall of man, the First Adam, who allowed the curse of the generations to come, leading up to God's punishment in the story of Noah and the Great Flood that destroyed every human being that remained on earth because of their unbelief.

After replenishing the earth and dividing the nations, God sought out a man by the name of Abram (later Abraham) with whom He made a covenant—but only after Abraham believed in God and did what He told him to do: Leave his family, friends, and home, and travel to the new land where God promised that he would be the father of a great nation and that his name would be great. Not only did God promise for this nation to be blessed, but other nations of the earth would also be blessed. Abraham's belief in God caused him to be obedient to the spirit of God. Even at age 75, Abraham's faith gave him the strength to depart from Haran and follow the spirit of God into the promised land of Canaan.

Out of Abraham came the nation of Israel, chosen to follow God and influence others. But they separated themselves from God and were made to wander in the wilderness for 40 years because of their unbelief. Along the way, they murmured, moaned, groaned, complained, spoke against Moses, and taunted God, even worshipping false idols. A God who brought them out of all their failure to a life of faith in Him.

"The fear of the LORD is the beginning of knowledge:
but fools despise wisdom and instruction."

— (Proverbs 1:7)

Don't do that! Don't complain about what you don't have, don't worry about things you don't see in the natural world, and don't let worry drown out your prayer life. When we understand that the fear of God is the beginning of knowledge, we can hold fast to the blessings of Abraham. Because God made his name great, 72 generations of a family tree—all the way down to the Savior of the world, Jesus Christ, Who came into the world that we might believe and that we might have abundance in life and love.

It's time to subdue ourselves in GOD. It's time to live out the dominion God gave to us. He gave us the more!

Encourage Yourself: I have the more—but only if I believe! Out of your belly shall flow rivers of living water—but only if you believe! Out of my belief comes the blessings of Abraham; he gave me the more.

"Now faith is the substance of things hoped for, the
evidence of things not seen."

— (Hebrews 11:1)

"Trust in the LORD with all thine heart; and lean not
unto thine own understanding. In all thy ways
acknowledge him, and he shall direct thy paths."

— (Proverbs 3:5-6).

I Have the More because I Believe!

Tekisha D Wimbush

_____

_____

_____

_____

_____

_____

_____

_____

_____

_____

_____

_____

_____

_____

_____

_____

_____

_____

_____

_____

_____

_____

_____

_____

_____

_____

_____

_____

_____

_____

_____
_____
_____
_____
_____
_____
_____
_____
_____
_____
_____
_____
_____
_____
_____
_____
_____
_____
_____
_____
_____
_____
_____
_____
_____
_____
_____
_____
_____
_____

THERE WAS A CAUSE FOR THE MOVEMENT
OF GOD TO COME DOWN TO EARTH, TAKE
THE NAME OF JESUS, BE WRAPPED IN

SWADDLING CLOTHES, AND BE LAID IN A MANGER

"Out of my belief comes blessings. "

Chapter 24
My God is a Progressive God: Let's Move Forward

Romans 3:25-26; Luke 24:10

progressive (adj) (google.com): (1) happening or developing gradually or in stages; proceeding step by step; (2) (of a group, person, or idea) favoring or implementing social reform or new, liberal ideas

W hen we look at the word "progressive," we get a sense of continuous growth, an increase in development, and constant elevation. To be progressive is to strive to move forward constantly. Our God is a God of movement! We are talking about a God of forward progress! This tells us that we must always be forward-thinking. Philippians 2:5 states,

> *"Let this mind be in you, which was also in Christ Jesus."*

This suggests movement: God moved to take on the natural form of man, Jesus, to understand man's sins and fulfill God's salvation plan. In our lesson text from Romans, Paul writes,

> *"Whom God hath set forth to be a propitiation through faith in his blood, to declare his righteousness for the remission of sins that are past, through the forbearance of God."*

— (Romans 3:25)

He did it just for me! Although God had a right to be justifiably angry with sinners, He showed us mercy, covered us in the blood of Jesus, and gave His only begotten Son so that we may have a right to the tree of Life (cf. John 3:16).

My God is a progressive God: let's move forward!

Everything has a cause and an effect. When we look at movement, we understand that there are measurable outcomes to validate the effects of a change. There was a cause for the movement of God to come down to earth, take the name of Jesus, be wrapped in swaddling clothes, and be laid in a manger. Owing to the effect of man's sins, which led to man's falling away from God, He sent his only begotten Son to redeem man and to reconcile man unto Him by atonement via the shedding of blood. This progressive movement through the plan of salvation is what we call reconciliation. Failure was not an option! Because there is no failure in God, we know that failure is a natural state of being finite, of failing to plan for our eternity.

I will follow the infinite Man, the I AM, the one true and wise God, who came to us as the Man with the plan. I live in the scripture, believing in Jesus—that He was bruised for my iniquity and died for my sins, and then He rose again so that I might live.

My God is a progressive God: let's move forward!

God set a plan in motion to show us forward progress through the movement of salvation. Following His death and burial, there was a resurrection. He arose with all power; He made Himself known to Mary Magdalene, Joanna, Mary the mother of James, and other women there. They then told these things to the apostles—they had to tell somebody about Jesus and that he yet lives!

Because God is a God of progression and has given us power through the blood of Jesus, we must not find ourselves sitting idly by. Instead, we must always find ourselves being "about our Father's business" moving forward. Tell someone about Jesus and how God loved us so that he gave up His only son. We must find ourselves spreading the good news of Jesus Christ and how He covered us in His blood. Tell someone about Jesus and how He saves, heals, delivers, and sets us free, rallying for the name of The Lord!

My God is a progressive God: Let's move forward!

_____
_____
_____
_____
_____
_____
_____
_____
_____
_____
_____
_____
_____
_____
_____
_____
_____
_____
_____
_____
_____
_____
_____
_____

> THERE WAS A CAUSE FOR THE MOVEMENT OF GOD TO COME DOWN TO EARTH, TAKE THE NAME OF JESUS, BE WRAPPED IN SWADDLING CLOTHES, AND BE LAID IN A MANGER

"We must find ourselves spreading the good news."

Chapter 25
Praise is Usual (My Praise); It's not Uncommon

Matthew 21:1-11

Matthew was a despised tax collector of his time—until he was chosen to become one of Jesus Christ's apostles. Having borne witness to the Son of God, he wrote the Book of Matthew not merely to give a chronological account of events but to present clear evidence that Jesus is the Messiah, Who links the Old and New Testaments as He is the fulfillment of the prophecies of the former.

"Think not that I am come to destroy the law, or the prophets: I am not come to destroy, but to fulfill."

— (Matthew 5:17).

praise (n) (dictionary.com): the act of expressing approval or admiration; commendation; laudation

> bless (vt) (dictionary.com): (1) to consecrate or sanctify by a religious rite; make or pronounce holy; (2) to extol as holy; glorify

We see in the prophets throughout the Old Testament a pattern regarding the coming of the Messiah, the chosen one the Jews waited upon to come and save them from Roman oppression. After years of preaching, teaching, healing, forgiving sins, and performing many miracles, Jesus rides into Jerusalem on a donkey, representing both his human and divine nature. However, to some, this was not the Messianic king they had envisioned. But things are not always as they appear!

> *"8 And a very great multitude spread their garments in the way; others cut down branches from the trees, and strawed them in the way.*
> *9 And the multitudes that went before, and that followed, cried, saying, Hosanna to the Son of David: Blessed is he that cometh in the name of the Lord; Hosanna in the highest."*
>
> — (Matthew 21:8-9)

Let's focus on this moment when Jesus' glory was recognized on earth. He was blessed and praised for coming to deliver God's people from bondage, from sin, from their oppressors, and from themselves. "Hosanna in the highest!" There was no time for doubt at that moment; even in the midst of their oppression, they praised God.

I have no time to choreograph my praise, no time to coordinate my rhythm, no time to make sure my feet shuffle together, and no time to see who's watching me. But right in the midst of my adversity, in the midst of my oppression, in the midst of my dilemma, I recognize my

Savior. I grab hold of my deliverance. And I break forth in praise. Praise is what I do whatever I'm going through! Right!

> *"My soul shall make her boast in the LORD: the*
> *humble shall hear thereof, and be glad."*
>
> — (Psalms 34:2)

Praise is Usual (My Praise); It's not Uncommon

It's in the name of Jesus

What's in a name? When we refer to the simple word that is a name, we think about how it is used to characterize individuals, whether good or bad depending on the situation. Many have had a falling out with certain individuals about calling them something other than their right name. We have had to correct people about our name's spelling and pronunciation. Some of us have even answered to the wrong name. For some, their name has made them prosperous; the mere mention of their name opens doors that would otherwise be closed. For others, hard times have followed their name. Some may have even changed their name to befit their lifestyle, employment, or career.

We all must know our names and the meaning behind who we are. You cannot address me improperly, out of my name, and expect it not to be an issue. I want to honor my name, what it stands for, and the beliefs it encompasses. I want my name to reflect the Name I belong to, for He promised to make my name great. It is only through the name of Jesus that we prosper and communicate with the Father.

> *"I am the way, the truth, and the life: no man cometh*
> *unto the Father, but by me."*
>
> — (John 14:6)

A name holds power, most of all the Name that is above all names:

> "9 *Wherefore God also hath highly exalted him, and*
> *given him a name which is above every name: 10*
> *That at the name of Jesus every knee should bow,*
> *of things in heaven, and things in earth, and things*
> *under the earth; 11 And that every tongue should*
> *confess that Jesus Christ is Lord, to the glory of*
> *God the Father"*
>
> — (Philippians 2:9-11)

For he is the light of the world (cf. John 8:12), and those that follow him shall not walk in darkness but shall have the light of life. Isaiah, son of Amos, understood this as well:

> "*Therefore the Lord himself shall give you a sign;*
> *Behold, a virgin shall conceive, and bear a son,*
> *and shall call his name Immanuel.*"
>
> — (Isaiah 7:14)

Isaiah went on to prophesy about the coming messiah to deliver us from darkness:

> "*For unto us a child is born, unto us a son is given: and*
> *the government shall be upon his shoulder: and his*
> *name shall be called Wonderful, Counsellor, The*
> *mighty God, The everlasting Father, The Prince of*
> *Peace.*"
>
> — (Isaiah 9:6)

Isaiah goes on to speak out and call the nation of Judah back to God and to tell of God's coming messiah, who shall be called:

- Wonderful, for He is exceptional and distinguished, and there is nobody like Him;
- Counselor, for He gives good advice;
- The mighty God, for he is God Himself manifested in the flesh;
- The everlasting Father, for He is God our timeless Father, Who instituted time itself;
- The Prince of Peace, for He is one government of peace: "And the peace of God, which passeth all understanding, shall keep your hearts and minds through Christ Jesus (Philippians 4:7).

It is all in the name of Jesus!

The book of Matthew was written to record proof that Jesus is the Messiah about Whom Isaiah prophesied. It's in His genealogy: Jacob begat Joseph, the husband of Mary, of whom Jesus was born, who is called Christ. Having been visited by an angel, Joseph was told to name Mary's baby Jesus—which means "Yahweh saves"—for He would save the people from their sins. Jesus is the descendant of the Jews and the savior of the Gentiles. It is in the name of Jesus that we have our liberty. It is in the name of Jesus that I have my salvation. Calling upon the name of Jesus saved me from my sins.

There is power in the name of Jesus!

_____

_____

_____

_____

_____

Tekisha D Wimbush

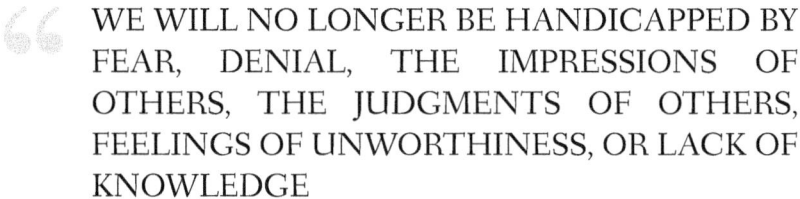

WE WILL NO LONGER BE HANDICAPPED BY FEAR, DENIAL, THE IMPRESSIONS OF OTHERS, THE JUDGMENTS OF OTHERS, FEELINGS OF UNWORTHINESS, OR LACK OF KNOWLEDGE

"Calling upon the name of Jesus saved me from my sins."

Chapter 26
Man Closes Doors, But So Do You

door (n) (dictionary.com): a movable, usually solid, barrier for opening and closing an entrance way, cupboard, cabinet, or the like, commonly turning on hinges or sliding in grooves

metaphor (n) (dictionary.com): a figure of speech in which a term or phrase is applied to something to which it is not literally applicable in order to suggest a resemblance, as in "A mighty fortress is our God."

What should we do when doors are closed that we feel should be open? Avenues in life that we feel entitled to can sometimes lead to detours, closed roads, and dead ends. However, it is often the case that the man that closed the doors is you! Point to yourself and say, "Me!" The early church in Laodicea allowed themselves to become complacent in their perceived wealth and the pleasures of this world. They started to fall away from God, closing the door to Him because of their temporal lusts. Of course, we know that only what you do for Christ will last!

In this sense, a door is usually referred to metaphorically rather than literally; e.g., a "door" can represent a particular life pathway. These doors can metaphorically be a relationship with God, blessings, healthy relationships, jobs, career opportunities, car sales, mortgage loans, educational degrees, business opportunities such as investments or new clients, grants, or even preaching engagements. A door leading to the ministry of the gospel of Jesus Christ was closed off to me simply because I was born female!

Man closes doors, but so do you!

For a very long time, I closed the door of accepting what God had planned for me to do. "I'm not where I used to be; I am progressing to where God has planned for me!" We are leaving out the "I'm not where I should be"; we will no longer make excuses in God. We will no longer be handicapped by fear, denial, the impressions of others, the judgments of others, feelings of unworthiness, or lack of knowledge—all stemming from low faith and lack of trust in God, low self-esteem, and lack of confidence, even though He called me! But one day, a speaker pierced my heart via the anointing of God. Having been thus outstretched, I lay in my tears and communicated one-on-one with God. I accepted God's will and surrendered myself unto His mighty hands. I opened the door that He left open all along, and I closed the door to my former self.

We often stunt our own growth and squander our own blessing, shutting our own doors to God in the process. "But how?" someone might ask. Or perhaps "No, not me?" Yes, you! Many of us know we should be further than where we are in life, especially when it comes to life in God. Leaning on our own understanding prohibits us and thwarts our progress. Today we understand that we are leaving out the "I'm not where I should be"; we will no longer make excuses in God. Repeat.

_____
_____
_____
_____
_____
_____
_____
_____
_____
_____
_____
_____
_____
_____
_____
_____
_____
_____
_____
_____
_____
_____
_____
_____
_____
_____
_____
_____

MY NAME IS NO LONGER DEFEATED; I AM NOW VICTORIOUS. MY NAME IS NO LONGER FEAR; I AM NOW POWER AND MIGHT.

Tekisha D Wimbush

"I opened the door — one that He left open all along."

Chapter 27
God Changed My Name

Isaiah is one of the most important prophets in the Old Testament. He had a zeal and a compassion for the people and desired to see the work of salvation manifested in their lives. Isaiah went into prayer for Jerusalem:

> "1 For Zion's sake will I not hold my peace, and for
> Jerusalem's sake I will not rest, until the
> righteousness thereof go forth as brightness, and
> the salvation thereof as a lamp that burneth.
> 2 And the Gentiles shall see thy righteousness, and all
> kings thy glory: and thou shalt be called by a new
> name, which the mouth of the LORD shall name"
>
> — (Isaiah 62:1-2).

name (n) (dictionary.com): a word or a combination of words by which a person, place, or thing, a body or class, or any object of thought is designated, called, or known

After God named the four rivers—Pison, Gihon, Hiddekel, and Euphrates (cf. Genesis chapter 2)—the first act of man (Adam) was to name all the living things that He created. But there was not a suitable helper for Adam! So God fashioned one out of one of Adam's ribs; he then proceeded to name his new companion "woman." Later, after Adam fell to sin, God allowed him to name the woman Eve, as she was the mother of all living things.

Later in Genesis, God gave a promise to a man named Abram. During this process, God renamed him Abraham and decreed that he shall be the father of many nations. God established a covenant with him and his future generations to always be their God. Then God also renamed Abraham's wife, Sarai, to Sarah, as she would be the mother of many nations and kings.

As a result of this covenant, God named for himself a holy people:

> *"For thou art an holy people unto the LORD thy God:*
> *the LORD thy God hath chosen thee to be a*
> *special people unto himself, above all people that*
> *are upon the face of the earth"*

> — (Deuteronomy 7:6).

Sin, iniquity, and transgressions separate us from God. The Lord will not forsake us; instead, we are the ones who forsake God when we sin:

> *"6 For the LORD hath called thee as a woman*
> *forsaken and grieved in spirit, and a wife of youth,*
> *when thou wast refused, saith thy God.*
> *7 For a small moment have I forsaken thee; but with*
> *great mercies will I gather thee.*
> *8 In a little wrath I hid my face from thee for a*
> *moment; but with everlasting kindness will I*

have mercy on thee, saith the LORD thy
Redeemer."

— (Isaiah 54:6-8).

God changed my name! Let's bring it home. They don't call me "Lil Kisha" anymore; I am now Lady K. They don't call him "Wet Out Willie" anymore; I am now Pastor Willie J. Wimbush Jr. They no longer call me crackhead, weed head, thot, liar, drunk. I am no longer an alcoholic; my name is now Sober and Vigilant. My name is no longer Defeated; I am now Victorious. My name is no longer Fear; I am now Power and Might. My name is no longer Bum; I am now Royalty, and I am part of a royal priesthood!

> *"4 To whom coming, as unto a living stone, disallowed*
> *indeed of men, but chosen of God, and precious,*
> *5 Ye also, as lively stones, are built up a spiritual*
> *house, an holy priesthood, to offer up spiritual*
> *sacrifices, acceptable to God by Jesus Christ.*
> *6 Wherefore also it is contained in the scripture,*
> *Behold, I lay in Sion a chief corner stone, elect,*
> *precious: and he that believeth on him shall not be*
> *confounded.*
> *7 Unto you therefore which believe he is precious: but*
> *unto them which be disobedient, the stone which*
> *the builders disallowed, the same is made the head*
> *of the corner,*
> *8 And a stone of stumbling, and a rock of offence, even*
> *to them which stumble at the word, being*
> *disobedient: whereunto also they were appointed.*
> *9 But ye are a chosen generation, a royal priesthood, an*
> *holy nation, a peculiar people; that ye should shew*
> *forth the praises of him who hath called you out of*
> *darkness into his marvellous light:*

> 10 *Which in time past were not a people, but are now the people of God: which had not obtained mercy, but now have obtained mercy."*

— (1 Peter 2:4-10)

What Is Your Name? Since God Changed You.

_____

_____

_____

_____

_____

_____

_____

_____

_____

_____

_____

_____

_____

_____

_____

_____

_____

_____

_____

_____

_____

_____

_____
_____
_____
_____
_____
_____
_____
_____
_____
_____
_____
_____
_____
_____
_____
_____
_____
_____
_____
_____
_____
_____
_____
_____
_____
_____
_____
_____
_____
_____

 IF GOD BE FOR US, WHO CAN BE AGAINST US?"

Chapter 28
The Only Thing That Stands between Me and Victory Is Me

Name: VICTORY

victory (n) (dictionary.com): a success or superior
position achieved against any opponent,
opposition, difficulty, etc.

Romans 8:31: "What shall we then say to these
things? If God be for us, who can be against us?"

W hat deters YOU from being victorious?

What does it mean to live victoriously?

Revelations 2:7: "He that hath an ear, let him hear
what the Spirit saith unto the churches; To him
that overcometh will I give to eat of the tree of life,
which is in the midst of the paradise of God."

Sometimes victories are short-lived, e.g., in cases where the victorious fail to remain engaged and strategic when facing opposition. An excellent example of this is celebrating too early. Failing to remain sensitive to the spirit of God leaves room in our hearts for the devil's wiles.

> *Negativity often robs us of our victory. Let us take a moment and review how the children of Israel almost allowed negativity to undo their God-given victory*
>
> — (cf. Deuteronomy 1:23-40)

> *Often the victorious also fail to plan for the temptation that follows the victory.*
>
> — (cf. Judges 15:18)

Pastor Wimbush stated, "Familiarity breeds laziness." What are your thoughts as you reflect on what it takes to maintain your victoriousness?

The victorious who remain faithful and loyal to Christ obtain a great reward.

> *Revelation 21:7: "He that overcometh shall inherit all things; and I will be his God, and he shall be my son."*

> *Romans 8: 37: "Nay, in all these things we are more than conquerors through him that loved us."*

Tekisha D Wimbush

_____

_____

"Negativity often robs us of our victory."

About the Author

Pastor Tekisha D. Wimbush M. ED., MSW, LSW is a native of Cleveland, Ohio, a Minister of the Gospel of Jesus Christ is the wife of Bishop Willie J. Wimbush Jr. Church of the Reform Church of Love in Cleveland, Ohio. Lady Wimbush's commitment to serving and helping others is evident through her lifestyle of service and dedication to the families and communities she serves. She diligently works with the Women's Ministry at the Church of the Reform Church of Love to promote unity and sisterhood. She frequently hosts prayer and Women's Forum meetings, retreats, workshops, and other events to empower women to develop and grow in the love of God. Lady Wimbush is an Author of the book entitled "The I AM in Me" she further, alongside her husband, serves in various ministries within The Church of the Reform, which include Adult Sunday School Teacher, Church Finance/ Administration Committee, Praise Team Leader, Engagement / Program Coordinator, Youth Ministry, and Outreach.

Lady Wimbush has a 15-year career history of employment with a Social Service agency in Cleveland, Ohio, where she supervised for over seven years. Lady Wimbush has previous experience as a hospice medical social worker at a Cleveland Hospice Agency and currently provides Clinical Counseling at an Independence Counseling Agency. With a Master's Degree in Social Work, a Master's Degree in Early Childhood Education, and a Bachelor's Degree in Business Administration and Social Science, Lady

Wimbush has a heart that resonates with restoring family relationships in a holistic modality. With all her accomplishments, she considers supporting her husband in ministry and raising God-fearing children her primary purpose. As a mother of three and grandmother of two, she firmly affirms that the best way to raise successful children is to be an active role model in demonstrating the love and fear of the Lord, which is the beginning of Wisdom.

www.ingramcontent.com/pod-product-compliance
Lightning Source LLC
Chambersburg PA
CBHW071326120626
46546CB00002B/463